Father Dolly

ADC to the Governor of Malta, 1921

Father Dolly

The Guardsman Monk

*The Memoirs of
Captain the Right Reverend
Dom Rudesind Brookes
OBE MC TD OSB,
Titular Abbot of Sherborne,
sometime Irish Guards, monk of Downside,
and Army and Royal Air Force Chaplain*

as narrated to Anthony Wheatley

HENRY MELLAND · London

DEDICATION

I dedicate these Memoirs to my dear half-sister, Claire, to all my brethren and former brethren at Downside and at her two daughter Houses, and to my friends of All Ranks, past and present, in my Regiment, the Irish Guards.

First published in Great Britain
by Henry Melland Limited
23 Ridgmount Street, London WC1E 7AH
1983

Designed by Norman Reynolds

ISBN 0 907929 04 4

Set in 11/12½ point Times
Printed in Great Britain by
The Eastern Press Limited, London and Reading

Contents

Acknowledgments

First and foremost I wish to thank Anthony Wheatley and his dear wife, Annette, for all their help in preparing these Memoirs, for putting me up in London many times in the past two years, and for arranging meetings with many old friends so that we could share memories of long ago.

Secondly, I would like to thank Colonel James Baker, the Regimental Lieutenant Colonel of the Irish Guards, for his active support and for so kindly reading these Memoirs with a view to accuracy of the military parts; and Major Robin Bullock-Webster, the Regimental Adjutant, and Orderly Room Quartermaster Sergeant O'Neill for their enormous help in checking the archives at Regimental Headquarters. I would also like to thank General Sir Basil Eugster KCB KCVO CBE DSO MC, the Colonel of the Regiment, who read the manuscript and made some very helpful comments.

Thirdly, I must thank Dom Philip Jebb, the Headmaster of Downside and the Monastic Archivist, who has not only been a tremendous help in delving into the monastic archives but also in checking the manuscript for accuracy of the monastic parts.

Next I would like to thank Colonel Richard Bird and Major J. Kenny of the Queen's Lancashire Regiment for all their trouble in providing me with information from their records about my service with the South Lancashire Regiment more than sixty years ago.

For much useful information about my first visit to Malta, I must thank my old friend and fellow ADC, Colonel H. F. Law DSO OBE MC TD, who so kindly sent me extracts from his then unpublished memoirs; and for checking what I have written about the Knights of Malta, I must thank Major General The Rt Hon The Viscount Monckton of Brenchley CB OBE MC.

I also wish to thank all those old friends whom I have visited or corresponded with in preparing these Memoirs. Firstly, my dear half-sister, Claire; and then Major James Lovegrove of the South Lancashire Regiment. From my early days with the Irish Guards: Colonel T. H. H. Grayson OBE, Major Sir Derrick Gunston Bt MC, Lieutenant Colonel Sir Kenneth Hogg Bt OBE, Captain J. B. Keenan, Lieutenant Colonel C. E. Maturin-Baird, Captain The Rt Hon The Earl of Munster and Brigadier J. O. E. Vandeleur DSO. From the monastery: Dom Denis Agius, Dom Clement Hayes, Dom Matthew Kehoe, Dom Adrian Morey, Dom Bernard Orchard, Dom Eric Phillips, Dom Hubert van Zeller and Dom Simon van Zeller. From the Second World War: Major Sir Oliver Chesterton Kt MC, Major David Drummond, Major J. T. Egan, Major Sir George FitzGerald Bt MC, Knight of Kerry, Brigadier D. M. L. Gordon-Watson OBE MC, Captain T. C. Keigwin MC, Lieutenant Colonel J. J. Kelly OBE, Major The Rt Hon The Lord Rawlinson of Ewell PC QC, Major W. I. Rooney MBE MM, Major B. T. Synge, Brigadier H. L. S. Young DSO, Garrison Sergeant Major George Stone MVO MBE, and last but not least my driver, dear Jack Ramsey of the Royal Army Service Corps. From my time as Parish Priest at Beccles: Mr John Trafford; and from my second visit to Malta two of the Governors, Admiral Sir Guy Grantham GCB CBE DSO, and Sir Maurice Dorman GCMG GCVO. In particular I would like to thank Sir Guy for writing such a very kind Foreword to this book. From my time in Rome: Mr Desmond Crawley CMG CVO, the British Minister to the Holy See, and his charming wife, Daphne; and from Colwich Abbey: The Right Reverend Dame Edith Street, now the Lady Abbess.

Finally, I would like to say how grateful I am to Pat Bowen, whose firm so kindly undertook to publish this book at bare cost provided there were enough subscribers. Pat not only served in the Irish Guards but was one of my boys at Downside when I was Housemaster of Roberts.

JRB

Foreword

by
Admiral Sir Guy Grantham GCB CBE DSO,
Commander-in-Chief, Mediterranean Fleet (1954–57),
Governor and Commander-in-Chief, Malta (1959–62)

This book is the story of the active life of a very exceptional man. I have read it with very great interest and enjoyment and I am sure many others will, through reading it, appreciate the many stirling qualities of Father Dolly, as he is affectionately known.

One does not often meet anyone who has had as many occupations and appointments as he has had, and who has made such a great success of each one he has undertaken.

I value very much his friendship over the last twenty-five or more years, and I admire greatly all he has achieved through his great interest in human beings of all ages and walks of life, his kindness, his loyalty to those with whom he served, both as a Guards officer, priest, headmaster and Abbot, and his unfailing sense of humour. He has made life happier for so many.

Guy Grantham

Citation for the Military Cross

CF 4th Class (Acting CF 3rd Class) Dom Rudesind BROOKES
OSB

1st Bn Irish Guards

Father Brookes has been the chaplain attached to this Bn ever since it came abroad. He has now served in both the Tunisian and Italian campaigns. In both these campaigns he has shown almost unbelievable devotion to duty and bravery. No wounded or dying man wherever he may be, has gone without Father Brookes' attention. He has been in places where the fire was impossibly heavy and yet he has given comfort to the dying without any thought for his own safety. During the last few weeks, in probably the fiercest fighting the British Army has yet seen, this Priest moved through shot and shell never appearing too tired to go to the furthest points to help a wounded man. He acted as the MO's assistant and on many occasions helped the stretcher bearers in their dangerous tasks of carrying men in. There are not words strong enough to describe the wonderful and shining example Father Brookes gave to all ranks, and all the officers and men of this Battalion would give testimony to the tireless kindliness, inspiration and help they all received from his hand. His personal bravery in addition to his priestly qualities gained him the admiration of all. The sight of Father Brookes pacing up and down reading his breviary under heavy fire has restored the confidence of many a shaken man.

In recognition of this Chaplain's extreme gallantry and unsparing devotion to duty, I recommend he be awarded the Military Cross.

9th March 1944

C.A. Montagu-Douglas-Scott
Lieutenant Colonel
Officer Commanding 1st Bn Irish Guards

Author's Preface

Through no merit of my own, I have been blessed by God with a long, varied and interesting life; and it is for that reason that I am putting pen to paper before it is too late.

At the outset I should make it clear that my life has not been typical of that of a Benedictine monk. Many of my brethren served as Chaplains during the two world wars but on the cessation of hostilities they returned to Downside and settled down once more to monastic life. As we shall see, in my case there were exceptional circumstances which resulted in my being absent from my monastery for very many years during and after the Second World War, only returning there on my final retirement.

Without any doubt there have been two great influences in my life: first and foremost my vocation as a priest and monk at the monastery of St Gregory the Great at Downside; and, coming a very close second, the Irish Guards, my Regiment in two world wars and in peace.

These Memoirs may therefore be of particular interest to my brethren in the monastic communities at Downside and at Ealing and Worth her two daughter houses, and to my very many friends of all ranks in the Irish Guards; but, because of the period covered and the events in which I was involved, I think that they may also be of interest to a much wider public. For that reason I have assumed that my readers are neither monks nor guardsmen; and I have tried to describe some of the technical background of both Benedictine monasticism and the Brigade of Guards which would not be common knowledge to the general reader. I trust therefore that both my brethren in the monastery and my many friends in the Footguards will bear with me when I describe matters which are well known to them.

In the earlier part of my story covering the period before the Second World War, I have tried to paint a picture of life in those days. It is a society and way of life which has virtually disappeared for ever; and therefore perhaps of interest to modern readers. There is certainly as much change in the life of a present day young Guards officer as in that of a present day young novice at Downside.

I am now 85 years of age, and like many old men, my memory is not what it was. However, with the help of my dear friend, Anthony Wheatley, who was in the school at Downside when I was a Housemaster and also served for a few years in the Irish Guards at the end of the war, I have had fascinating meetings with the surviving members of my noviciate, with very many 'Micks' of all ranks who knew me at various periods of my career, and with two of the four Governors of Malta under whom I had the privilege of serving. I have therefore been able to confirm my memories with theirs; and, while I apologise to readers for any errors of detail in my general descriptions, I can promise that every incident described has been confirmed and substantiated by the memories of other people beside myself.

Downside, 25th March 1983
Feast of the Annunciation of Our Lady

JRB

My mother

Chapter 1

Early Days

I was born in London on 14th March, 1898. Many of my friends think of me as a typical Englishman, but that is far from the truth. My real name is Count John Charles Hugo de Minciaky, a fact of which I remained ignorant until the age of sixteen.

My father, Count Emile Maria de Minciaky, was a Russian from Georgia, a Roman Catholic, and at the time of my birth an Attaché at the Imperial Russian Embassy to the Court of St James, which was then in St Petersburg Square, Bayswater.

My mother, Beatrix, was Swedish and a Lutheran, her father being Eric Hugo Waldenstrom; but her mother, Elizabeth Hannaway, was Irish. I am therefore half Russian, a quarter Swedish and a quarter Irish.

My parents were married on 27th August 1892, by Father Frederick Antrobus at the Brompton Oratory. They were subsequently divorced and my mother married Warwick Brookes in 1900 and later bore him a daughter, my half-sister Claire, some three years after my own birth.

My stepfather, whose father and grandfather were also christened Warwick after the Earls of Warwick to whom they were distantly related, was a very extrovert flamboyant character whose finances fluctuated alarmingly. He was in business and had an iron-foundry in Essex. Later, during the War, he went into politics for a short time. He was an inveterate gambler with expensive tastes; and, although at times he had been a very wealthy man, he died almost bankrupt. Although he was in fact my stepfather, throughout my childhood and youth I believed him to be my own father.

When Claire was born we were living at Bedford Court Mansions in Bedford Street. Quite early on we acquired a Nanny, whom we dearly loved, who was known as Aunt Emma and her husband was Uncle Sam. When I was about six, we were boarded out with Aunt Emma and Uncle Sam and went to live in a small village in Derbyshire called Doveholes near Buxton. The station must have been on the main line from Manchester to London, as I have a vivid memory of being taken with Claire to stand on the platform and wave to my mother when she passed through on the London express and waved back to us from a carriage window.

To the modern reader this may sound rather callous behaviour on the part of our parents and indeed it was certainly an unusual arrangement, but one must remember that in those days upper-class children were brought up by servants as a matter of course and were only brought down to the drawing room to see their parents for half an hour after tea each day. Presumably this arrangement left our parents more freedom for living their busy social lives.

When I was 10, we all returned to London to a house in Bedford Square. Two famous men living in the Square at that time were: Weedon Grossmith, who wrote *Diary of a Nobody* and Anthony Hope, famous for *The Prisoner of Zenda.* Later we moved to a flat at No 1, South Molton Street, Mayfair.

Soon after our return to London, I was sent to a school in Finchley where I remained for four years. It was an excellent school where I was very happy and I particularly remember that I had a wonderful history master who aroused an interest in his subject which has remained with me all my life. I was a day boy and used to travel to and fro by No 13 bus.

Warwick's great hobby was sailing and we often went to Burnham-on-Crouch in Essex for holidays where I learnt to sail small dinghies. Eventually I was given my own boat which I named *Peter Pan.* Sometimes Warwick took a small house for the season or he might just take rooms for us, as my mother did not share his enthusiasm for sailing and seldom accompanied us.

When I was 14, it was decided that I should go to public school and I was sent to Eastbourne College. No doubt Warwick was influenced in his choice of school by the fact that two of Lloyd George's sons were there at the time. My mother and stepfather took me down to meet the Headmaster and see round the school. When we were leaving, my stepfather asked the Headmaster which was the best hotel in the town. On being told that it was the famous Grand Hotel, he instructed the cabbie in the hearing of the Headmaster to take us to the Grand; but as soon as we had driven out of earshot he rapped on the window and redirected the taxi to a much less pretentious establishment. This was typical of Warwick; and it will not surprise readers when I tell them that two years later – half way through my schooling – Warwick could not pay the bill and had to withdraw me from the school.

My stepfather, Warwick Brookes

This brought my formal education to an abrupt halt and readers will rightly think that it had been minimal and to say the least unorthodox; but I had early acquired a great love for history and I like to think that my rather neglected childhood spurred me on to educate myself.

As I have related, my real father was a Roman Catholic and in accordance with the normal rules of the Catholic Church my mother, who was a Lutheran despite her Irish mother, had agreed that their children be brought up as Catholics in order to obtain dispensation to marry. However, as a result of the break-up of her first marriage I was not even baptised, nor was my half-sister, as Warwick was not a very religious man. As the years went by my mother's conscience must have pricked her because when I was nearly 14 she arranged for both of us to receive instruction from Father Gavin, a Jesuit at nearby Farm Street. In due course we were baptised at the Church of Our Lady of the Assumption in Warwick Street, as Farm Street was not a Parish Church; and we subsequently made our First Holy Communion at Farm Street. Shortly afterwards, we were confirmed at the Cathedral by the Cardinal Archbishop of Westminster.

When I was about 16, I was rummaging through some old family albums of my mother's when I came across a Family Tree of her family, the Waldenstroms. I studied it with interest and was suddenly galvanised by the realisation that the last entry, John de Minciaky, must be myself. I spoke about it to a maternal uncle who was living in London, but he refused to discuss the matter, so I made my own enquiries, first at the Russian Embassy where it was confirmed that Emile Maria de Minciaky had indeed been an Attaché at the time of my birth and secondly at the Brompton Oratory where the Register recorded my parents' marriage in 1892. Sadly, I was never able to trace my father after the Great War. He had left London soon after my birth but in the maelstrom of the Russian Revolution it was impossible to know whether he had survived or been slaughtered like so many other aristocrats.

Chapter 2

France

It is difficult to believe now that young men were desperately anxious not to miss the fighting in the First World War and tried to get themselves accepted when only 16 or 17. Yet it was indeed so. Soon after my abrupt departure from Eastbourne College, my thoughts naturally turned to joining up. Needless to say, Warwick wanted his stepson to join the Brigade of Guards and, as I was a Catholic and had Irish blood through my maternal grandmother, he suggested that I try for a commission in the Irish Guards. He had a certain amount of influence through his friends in the Carlton Club, and arranged to take me along to Regimental Headquarters for an interview with Colonel D.J. Proby, the Regimental Lieutenant Colonel. However, the latter was not impressed and told Warwick '. . . to send the boy back to school' but it was agreed that I might join when I was 18.

This was not good enough for me in 1915, with the possibility that the War might be over before I was 18, so Warwick used his influence with another high-ranking friend and in due course on 30th June, 1915, at the age of 17, I was commissioned into the 2nd/4th Battalion, South Lancashire Regiment (Prince of Wales' Volunteers).

They were stationed at Ashford in Kent and, having got my uniform and baggage, I took a train for Ashford and put up at the best hotel I could find. The next morning I found the Battalion Headquarters and reported to the Adjutant, just as the Battalion was about to set off on a route march. He told me to dump my baggage and fall in at the head of one of the platoons. Although I had been in the Officers' Training Corps at

17

Eastbourne College, I was filled with trepidation at being pitch-forked straight on parade. However, my Platoon Sergeant was a splendid type who immediately realised the situation. 'Don't worry, Sir. Just do what I tell you and you'll be all right.' And I was!

The Commanding Officer was Lieutenant Colonel J.D. Fairclough, and the Adjutant, under whom I came for discipline as a young officer, was Captain Peter Hacket. Although I had been so eager to join up, I little realised that by joining a Territorial Battalion I had ensured that I would not be sent to France immediately.

The Territorial Army's original role was Home Defence, taking over from the Regular Army which was thus free to be sent overseas as the British Expeditionary Force. Soon after war was declared, it was decided that each Territorial unit should expand by forming a 'second line' which was to be equipped and trained for service overseas. Unlike Kitchener's New Army, which was raised and sent overseas to reinforce the regulars very quickly and with very little training or experience, most of the Territorials did not get out to France until 1917 and thus missed the carnage of the Somme.

It was for this reason that the battalion, which had been formed in September 1914, was called the *2nd*/4th Bn; and it carried out training for the next two years, firstly at Ashford and later at Oxted and Blackdown. We were part of the 172nd Infantry Brigade, 57th Division.

Shortly after joining, I was sent on a General Course for Officers at Cambridge which lasted three months. In 1919 after the War was over, I was sent on a three month Education Course at Oxford. On neither occasion were we part of the university; but I like to say that I have been to both Oxford and Cambridge!

During 1916, I went on a Musketry Course at Aldershot where I became proficient in the working of the Lewis gun and obtained a 'Distinguished' pass. I also did an Anti-Gas Course at Tidworth where I qualified as 2nd Class Instructor.

At the beginning of the War my stepfather established a factory for the manufacture of war equipment such as canvas buckets, nosebags, ground sheets, etc. He had become Managing Director of both the Junior Army and Navy Stores and of the Civil Service Co-operative Society. When these two concerns were amalgamated his holding became so valuable that he received an offer of £50,000 for it, which he refused. Later, during the post-war slump, he disposed of it for less than half that sum.

In the 1916 election Warwick stood for Parliament as a Coalition Unionist and was duly elected the Honourable Member for Mile End. He was a strong supporter of the Government's conscription policy, which he contended should have included Ireland. He was immensely proud to have a son in uniform, and sometimes when I was on leave asked me to accompany him to political meetings and sit on the platform with him. This probably put the thought into my head of becoming a politician myself and later, when I was thinking of leaving the Army, I gave it serious consideration but, as we shall see, I decided against it.

At the end of 1916, Lieutenant Colonel T.H.S. Marchant of the 13th Hussars took over command of the Battalion and we were warned for active service. We eventually left Frith Hill Barracks at midnight on 15th February 1917, entraining at Frimley Station for Folkestone, and disembarking at Boulogne the following day. We then proceeded by train to a village near Hazebrouk where we were billeted in a farm and remained there several days before marching to Sailly-sur-Lys. Early the following morning we took over a line of trenches in the Bois Grenier sector, near Armentières.

The 57th Division remained in this area until October when it moved up into the Ypres Salient. During this time there were no major operations and I see that according to the Regimental History all was officially 'quiet'. However, this term is merely relative and as far as we were concerned the discomfort and danger of trench warfare was ever present. Few days passed without a casualty and we lived under conditions of exposure and general desolation that can be better imagined than described.

On 7th May we were in the line in the Rue du Bois sector and at about 7pm the gas alarm was raised by the troops on our left. Shortly afterwards a cloud of poisonous fumes passed over our trenches, but without causing any casualties, as we had all had ample time to don our respirators. However, just after midnight, the enemy opened up with their machine-guns and put down a trench-mortar and shrapnel barrage on our front line, prior to putting in an assault. The attacking infantry were in fact dispersed by our own artillery and Lewis-gun fire and the attack beaten off, but I was unaware of any of this, as I had been hit in the head by a piece of flying shrapnel. I had bent forward and so was hit in the neck under my shrapnel helmet; but I was extremely lucky for if the wound had been a few inches higher I would certainly have been killed. As it was, I was not even knocked unconscious, though I bled profusely, and I was able to walk back to our Regimental Aid Post from which I was despatched to the Field Ambulance and eventually to the Base Hospital at Calais. My wound did not merit return to England; but it was sufficiently serious to keep me several weeks in hospital and it was not until 22nd June that I rejoined the Battalion for duty. On 1st July, I was promoted Lieutenant, just two years after joining.

When we were in the line, we carried out patrols in No Man's Land and occasionally there were bigger raids to capture prisoners and so obtain enemy information. On 1st August such a raid was carried out by 'D' Company, Kenneth Gordon and I being the two subalterns in command. Amongst my papers I recently came across a page of the Orders issued for this raid which I reproduce below.

Right Support Line Parties	(g) *Lt Gordon* will take his party down the Right C.T., when the flanks of the Front Line have been blocked, dropping on the way L/Cpl Ball and Pte Warburton with their parties to hold the trenches on his right flank already indicated to him. He will direct the action of Sgt Taylor's party in mopping up the Support Line and Dugouts in the line immediately in rear, gaining touch eventually with the party under Lt Brookes.

Left Support Line Party	(h)	*Lt Brookes* will lead his party down the Left C.T. as soon as the Front Line has been satisfactorily blocked; on reaching the triangle where this C.T. meets the Support Line, he will take steps to rush and secure the two bombing posts which appear to defend this junction. L/Cpl Carey's party will hold the C.T. which continues towards the enemy rear lines at all costs. Sgt Woodward with his party will block and hold the trenches leading to the left, where dugouts are suspected from which the enemy may emerge. No attempt will be made to clear these dugouts until the remainder of the duties allotted to Lt Brookes have been carried out; then if time allows a strong party will be sent to clear them. Sgt Arrowsmith's party will mop up towards the parties under Lt Gordon in the Support Line and line of dugouts in rear, the larger portion being detailed for the latter duty.
Diversion	(i)	A party of 1 NCO and 6 men detailed by OC 'B' Coy and practised beforehand in the duty, will place dummy figures in NO MAN'S LAND about 100 yards in advance of CHARDS FARM SALIENT at a spot personally pointed out to him. These figures will be in position by 10.30pm on the night of the raid and they will be manipulated during the diversion, being pulled up and lowered for varying periods to attract the enemy's attention. The figures will be first raised at ZERO minus 3 min.
7 EQUIPMENT		All ranks taking part will black their faces and remove all identification marks such as identity discs, regimental badges and numerals, yellow arm badges, pay books,

private correspondence. No document, map or plan is to be taken into the attack.

A label with name, rank & religion, will be carried in the right breast pocket.

These labels will be given up to the tally officer on return from the raid.

Neither caps nor helmets will be worn. Goggles will be carried in the left side pocket.

Ammunition will be carried in the right side pocket: magazines will be charged in addition to what is laid down to be carried on the man.

Bayonets and other bright or light coloured articles will be painted a dark colour.

Articles with which individuals and parties are equipped are laid down in Appendices 'B' & 'C'.

8 PASS WORDS

No pass word will be employed, but parties will inform each other of the position by calling out their leader's name, which will be answered by the leader's name of other parties within hearing.

CT stood for Communication Trench. These went from front to rear more or less at right-angles to the Front Line. The Support Line was parallel to and some distance in rear of the Front Line and the Communication Trenches cut through the Support Line and gave access from the rear to both Support and Front Lines. It will thus be seen that Gordon and I had to take our parties down the two Communication Trenches opposite our sector and isolate the Front and Support Lines from our left and right while we took prisoners and brought them back.

In the event the raid was successful, two prisoners and valuable documents being taken, and several of the enemy killed. There was considerable fighting at close quarters and a number of decorations were awarded for this action. My own Sergeant

Woodward received the Military Medal for valour and devotion to duty.

Some of the subalterns being sent out as reinforcements at this time were very young indeed. One youngster who joined us shortly before I left the Battalion was James Lovegrove, a cherubic lad who was nicknamed 'Smiler'. Soon after joining he innocently confided in us that the previous day on a route march the troops had been singing 'A little child shall lead them'. As his Company Commander was on leave, we suggested that the following day he should parade his men in Full Marching Order and tell them that they were going on a 20-mile march and again a little child would lead them but this time he would be mounted on a horse! 'Smiler' carried out this plan and his announcement caused consternation among the troops. The Sergeant Major then asked him if he was ready to mount, to which he replied that it had only been a jape. However, the Sergeant Major then said: 'Oh you'll have to mount now, Sir, I'll help you on.' He then proceeded to 'help' 'Smiler' on right over the other side! 'Smiler' eventually managed to mount and trotted up to the head of his men. However, the Colonel must have been told because he had not gone a hundred yards before the Colonel's galloper caught up: 'The Colonel's compliments, Sir, and will you please dismount and report to him in the Orderly Room.' On arrival in the Orderly Room, Colonel Marchant, a distinguished cavalry officer, roared out: 'What on earth are you doing? You look like a sack of potatoes!' However, the joke rebounded on all us subalterns, as the Colonel made the lot of us go to Riding School after that while we were out of the Line.

On 26th October my Commission in the Irish Guards came through and I was transferred to the 2nd Battalion which was serving in the same sector. However, my new brother officers looked very much askance at a Territorial officer and immediately decided that I was not fit to fight with the Guards until I had completed a proper Drill Course for Young Officers, and I was therefore sent back to the Reserve Battalion which was stationed at Warley Barracks in Essex. I should add that I was dropped back to 2nd Lieutenant, or Ensign as it was and still is called in the Brigade.

When I arrived at Warley I had to get a complete change of uniform as in those days officers of Line Regiments wore their badges of rank on their sleeves rather like naval officers whereas in the Guards rank badges were worn on the shoulders as is the present custom throughout the Army.

Perhaps at this point I should write a few words about the constitution of and customs peculiar to the Brigade. Of course one has to admit that the very use of the latter term indicates unconscious superiority. There are many Brigades in the British Army, but I am sure no one would dispute that reference to 'The Brigade' can only mean the Brigade of Guards. The latter term was used to cover the whole of the Footguards as opposed for example to the Nth Guards Brigade which would be an operational unit composed of two or more Guards battalions. The Household Cavalry were entirely separate and it was not until 1968 that they came to be included with the Footguards in the Household Division. Up to that time they had their own Depot at Windsor and employed cavalry dismounted drill, which was incompatible with infantry drill.

My own Regiment was at that time of very recent origin. Queen Victoria's last public act in 1900 was to order the formation of an Irish Regiment of Footguards to commemorate the bravery of the Irishmen who had fallen in the South African War. It was formed by the transfer of Irishmen mostly from other Guards Regiments but also from throughout the Army. The Welsh Guards were of even more recent origin, having only been formed in 1915. As we shall see later, their very first Regimental Sergeant Major came out of retirement to Downside as Sergeant Major of the Officers' Training Corps during the Second War.

At the head of the Brigade of Guards is the Major General, who is also the General Officer Commanding London District with his Headquarters at the Horse Guards in Whitehall. He is responsible for the security of the Metropolis and for more than two centuries prior to the founding of the Metropolitan Police by Sir Robert Peel, the Footguards were employed to maintain law and order in a very rowdy London.

Under the Major General come the Regimental Lieutenant

Colonels commanding the five Regiments with their individual Headquarters in Birdcage Walk. These officers are full Colonels by rank and are responsible for recruiting both officers and men and for postings, records, etc. They jealously guard all regimental privileges and customs and woe betide any General, however senior, who may have Guardsmen under his command and who tries to infringe or curtail any of these customs. Each Regiment also has a Colonel who is either a member of the Royal Family, a Field Marshal or a distinguished General, while the Monarch is Colonel-in-Chief of all five Regiments.

The Monarch has always taken a close interest in the Brigade and sometimes makes a personal intervention. After the First War, moustaches went out of fashion, but after a time King George V considered that the clean-shaven Guardsmen looked too young and immature, so the edict went forth: 'Moustaches will be grown!' At the beginning of the Second War, the Army abandoned the old peaked Service Dress cap and adopted the Field Service cap, commonly known as the 'fore and aft' as it was perched on the side of the head. King George VI thought it too undignified for his Guardsmen, so an exception was made and throughout the War, while the rest of the Army went through a succession of different headgear, the Guardsmen continued to be immediately recognisable by their old-style Service Dress caps with the traditional 'Cheese-cutter' peaks. Going back before my time, it seems that Queen Victoria did not like seeing Non-commissioned officers of the Queen's Guard wearing the single chevron of a Lance Corporal, so all Lance Corporals in the Brigade wear two chevrons and are virtually indistinguishable from full Corporals.

Turning now to customs: I shall be referring to officers doing Picquet duty or being punished with Extra Picquets. In the Brigade the Picquet Officer and Picquet Sergeant are the equivalent of Orderly Officer and Orderly Sergeant in Line Regiments and are the officials on duty in barracks or camp outside working hours. Being part of the Court, the term 'in-waiting' is also used for being on duty, so each Company has a Sergeant-in-waiting, Corporal-in-waiting and Corporal-second-in-waiting, while at Battalion level there is a Drill Sergeant-in-waiting. Battalions of Footguards have the unique privilege of two additional senior Warrant Officers on their Establishments, known as Drill Sergeants, who assist the Regimental Sergeant Major and rank above the Company Sergeant Majors.

Customs in Officers' Messes vary enormously from one Regiment to another and while some are quite informal others are sticklers for seniority and even insist on subalterns addressing captains as 'Sir'. In the Brigade the basic principle is that everyone is equal in the Mess and therefore Christian names or nicknames are used, the only exception being the Commanding Officer who is addressed as 'Sir'. However, new young ensigns joining the Regiment have to be accepted in the Mess and can have quite a sticky time on first joining. If a young ensign had the audacity to speak to anyone other than a fellow ensign without first being spoken to, he would be likely to get a frosty reception. Years ago the period before acceptance might be as long as six months, but now it would probably not be more than a few weeks. There is a pleasant custom by which officers of the rank of Lieutenant Colonel and above are referred to by their rank coupled with their Christian names: thus one gets Colonel Andrew or Brigadier Joe or General Tim.

Another unusual custom was that of officers wearing their caps at breakfast in the Mess if they did not wish to be spoken to. Although it might appear rather eccentric, it was in fact quite sensible as it prevented some unwary young officer from wishing a cheery 'Good morning' to a hard-drinking major suffering from a hang-over!

At that time officers always travelled first class on the railway, whether in uniform or plain clothes. As it was a railway, we were also allowed to travel on the tube in London; but we were never allowed to travel on omnibuses. We were not allowed to carry parcels in the street, so if we went shopping the goods would have to be delivered or we would have to take our soldier servants with us to carry the parcels.

At Warley there must have been about twenty ensigns in training at the time I was there. Because of the number, although we ate with the other officers, we were not allowed in the main ante-room but had our own ensigns' ante-room.

Lieutenant Colonel Tom Vesey, who had been severely wounded in 1914, was our Commanding Officer. He had a habit of having the 'Officers' Call' sounded by the Duty Drummer, upon which we all had to rush to the Orderly Room where we would be ticked off or punished for our peccadilloes and even in some cases placed under arrest – though I am happy to say that did not happen to me!

Tim Nugent was the Adjutant, a job which he also had after the War with the 1st Battalion when it returned to England, so I was under him for two periods of my service. I also met Sidney FitzGerald for the first time at Warley. Sidney, who was always known as 'Black Fitz', had been wounded in France and was at that time a Company Commander. He became Adjutant of the 1st Battalion after the War just before it went out to Turkey and, as we shall see, I suffered greatly under him as Adjutant when I rejoined the Battalion after its return to England in 1924.

Sidney's ensigns had rather a rough time as he used to make them take their own Platoon Orders while he stood behind in the Company Office. Edgar Maturin-Baird, one of my fellow ensigns, told me how he had a man in the Report for breaking a window. At a loss what to do, he remanded the man for the Company Commander, whereupon Sidney broke in: 'You bloody fool. Deal with him yourself!' Fortunately, the Company Sergeant Major came to the rescue by whispering 'Pay for the repair' which Edgar repeated aloud.

One of my friends at that time was Eddie FitzClarence who later became the Earl of Munster. Eddie was a very debonair young blade and it is to him that I owe my nickname which he gave me and which I have had ever since. Up to that time I had usually been known as 'Brookie', but one day Eddie gave me a scurrilous book to read called *The Adventures of Dolly Varden*. I was not a prude and I certainly had no thought then of becoming a priest, but I had no time for that sort of book and I threw it down on the sofa, saying 'I can't waste my time reading that rubbish', whereupon Eddie exclaimed: 'Oh Dolly!' and the nickname stuck and has remained with me all my life. I am really very grateful to Eddie as everyone seemed to have a nickname in those days and some were not very complimentary. Kenneth

Hogg was for obvious reasons always known as 'Piggy', while Francis Law with whom I later served in Malta was for some more obscure reason known as 'Pokey', and there were many other such examples.

Francis had been wounded at Passchendaele and after recovering from his wounds arrived at Warley about the same time as myself. He was Field Training Officer and we Young Officers came under him for this part of our training, though he was not yet 21 and some of his pupils were older than him! We later served together in the 2nd Battalion in France, to which he was posted as a Company Commander about a month after I joined it.

On 20th March 1918, having completed my training, I was posted back to the 2nd Battalion in France. It was then that I first met Lieutenant Colonel the Hon Harold Alexander DSO MC, always known as 'Alex' and later to become Field Marshal, who was then commanding the battalion at the early age of 27. I only served under him for about six months at that time, then as we shall see for another three months in Constantinople in

Me, sailing over the water-jump at Warley, 1917

28

1922, and lastly for my final year in London before leaving the Army in 1925, yet we became life-long friends.

As a young officer, I was immediately impressed by his personality which, though a little reserved and aloof, was full of character, and quite frankly it had an originality which I have never met in anyone else. I felt immediately attracted to him and realised that I was in the presence of a real leader of men despite his youth – he was indeed one of the youngest officers ever to command a battalion in the Regiment. His originality was not in any way freakish or bizarre; it was just that he approached the very simple ordinary things in life in a way that was just a little bit different. He was a Protestant Ulsterman, yet very sympathetic to Catholicism and very much aware that the Regiment was a Catholic one. His faith and religion meant much to him and I cannot do better than quote from a letter written by him to a friend a few weeks before his death, which I think shows the very basis of what formed his character:

'If I may strike a personal note it is to say what a strength and comfort it was to me when, as a young subaltern in the Irish Guards during the First World War, I knelt with my men on the battlefield before the attack and received that spiritual support given to us all, both Protestant and Catholic, by our Regimental Chaplain.'

I do not think it is generally known that Alex carried a crucifix inside his uniform jacket throughout the Second World War. Knowing what close friends we had been, his widow very kindly gave me this crucifix as a keepsake after he died, and I have treasured it ever since. When a monk dies, all his personal possessions belong to the monastery, but the Abbot has readily agreed that an exception shall be made and after my death Alex's crucifix will be given to the Irish Guards.

I got back to France just in time for the last great German offensive, which started on the day after my arrival. As is well known, much of the hard-won territory of the Allies was overrun in a matter of days and there began a general retreat which almost developed into a rout, whole battalions and even brigades being cut-off.

We were in the 4th Guards Brigade and Colonel Alex had to

take command during the retreat from Arras as the Brigade Commander, Lord Ardee, had been gassed. Then at the beginning of April, the Brigade was ordered to fill a gap in the defence of Hazebrouck caused by the collapse of a Portuguese Division. We took up position near the village of Vieux Berquin, our battalion being in reserve; but there was no front line and no other troops on either flank – in fact we were the only troops standing between the Germans and the Channel Coast. We had to hang on at all costs until we could be relieved by the 1st Australian Division due to arrive at Hazebrouck within 36 hours. It was then that Sir Douglas Haig issued his famous Order of the Day: 'There is no course open to us but to fight it out. Every position must be held to the last man: there must be no retirement. With our backs to the wall, and believing in the justice of our cause, each one of us must fight on to the end.' With his usual humour, Alex commented: 'It's not backs to the wall for us: it's backs to back.' The losses of the whole brigade were simply appalling; but somehow we hung on until relieved by the Australians, and Haig subsequently wrote: 'The performance of all troops engaged in this most gallant stand, especially that of the 4th Guards Brigade, on whose front of some 4,000 yards the heaviest attacks fell, is worthy of the highest praise. No more brilliant exploit has taken place since the opening of the enemy's offensive, though gallant actions have been without number.'

After this successful defeat of the enemy's last great offensive, both our battalions had been so decimated that it proved impossible to supply reserves to keep both at fighting strength and it was decided that the 2nd Battalion should act as a feeder for the 1st Battalion. Our last big ceremonial parade was a distribution of medals by General Lord Plumer. Little did I know then that I was to be his ADC when he became Governor of Malta after the War. We then withdrew to Criel Plage near Dieppe where we remained until the Armistice. This did not mean that we thought the War was over; on the contrary we trained very hard and were so fit that we won every single event of the Brigade Sports. Among the officers who won events were Colonel Alex, Francis Law and myself. When the Armistice was finally announced, we could scarcely believe it.

News of the Armistice being read to the Irish Guards,
11th November 1918

Just before this, Colonel Alex left the Battalion to take command of the 10th Army School, which was a sad blow to us all –
officers and men alike. He subsequently served in Latvia where
he commanded an army of German Balts against the Bol-
sheviks, and it was not until 1920 that he rejoined the Regiment
as Second-in-Command of the 1st Battalion. Before leaving, he
issued the following message to All Ranks: 'In bidding you
farewell I wish to express to you all my sincere grief at leaving a
Battalion I am so fond of. We have been through some hard
times together, but the remembrance of those battles in which
the 2nd Battalion has taken such a glorious part will always be a
great pride to me. Remember the great name this wonderful
Battalion has made for itself in the War. Be proud of it and
guard it jealously. I leave you with complete confidence that its
reputation is safe in your hands. I thank you from the bottom of
my heart for the loyalty you have always shown me during the

31

whole time that I have had the honour of commanding you. I wish you all and individually the best possible luck and success, and a safe return to your homes when the War is over.'

In due course we set off by train with the rest of the 4th Guards Brigade and proceeded to Mauberge where we rejoined the Guards Division. From there we had to march to Germany on foot; and although there were one or two pleasant diversions such as a stop in a chateau at Presles where we laid on a boar shoot, it was a long and dreary journey. On 22nd December we entered Germany and entrained for Cologne, where we commenced the Occupation.

The men were quartered quite comfortably in a German Army barracks but, as there were no Officers' Messes in the German Army, the officers had to find billets in private houses. I hit upon the brainwave of billeting myself on the Curator of the Cologne Zoological Gardens. He had a fine house in the grounds of the Zoo and I was very comfortable. He had a pleasant matronly wife and an attractive young daughter; and a very embarrassing incident occurred shortly after I took up my

Cologne Cathedral and the Hohenzollern Bridge, 1919

Two Micks enjoying bully beef on the boat home

quarters there. Somehow I failed to lock the door of the 'loo' and I was caught with my trousers down when the young daughter burst in. However, from this rather unfortunate beginning we became very good friends.

Our duties consisted of street patrols, guards on food and ammunition dumps, bridges and railway yards; and of course a lot of time was devoted to bringing us back to peacetime standards of drill. In January 1919, the Prince of Wales came out to present us with our first Colours – having been formed in wartime, we had never had any Colours. It was a moving moment but sad as we knew that we were to be disbanded within

33

a few months and our new Colours would then be laid up. Incidentally, it may not be generally known that it was at that time, in order to commemorate the gallantry of his Guards Regiments, King George V decreed that private soldiers in the Footguards should henceforth be known as 'Guardsman' instead of 'Private'.

In February 1919, we returned to England and were stationed once again at Warley Barracks. On 22nd March the whole Guards Division took part in a great Victory Parade through London, the streets being lined by schoolboys from the Officers' Training Corps. Finally, on 31st March, the 2nd Battalion was disbanded and our newly-presented Colours were laid up in the Catholic church at the Guards Depot at Caterham. The following day I was transferred to the 1st Battalion which was also at Warley.

Chapter 3

Peacetime Soldiering

I had never intended to become a regular soldier and would perhaps have followed Warwick into politics, but I had come to enjoy the life and applied to become a regular. My commission as a Second Lieutenant was on the Supplementary Reserve of Officers and now, in April 1919, I was once more promoted Lieutenant but still on the SRO. It was not in fact until February 1921, that I was eventually granted a Regular Commission backdated to June 1919.

We returned to peacetime soldiering with Spring Drills for the Young Officers under one of the Drill Sergeants. In the summer we moved to Chelsea Barracks where we remained until September 1920, when we were sent down to Aldershot for six months.

At Chelsea we carried out Public Duties with occasional breaks at Purfleet or Pirbright for range work or manoeuvres. There was a lot of industrial unrest at that time and a series of strikes. In 1919 there was a rail strike and the troops were quartered at the HAC barracks in the City and the officers were billeted in considerable luxury at the Great Eastern Hotel in Liverpool Street. We had to mount guards on both Broad Street and Liverpool Street stations and on the Bishopsgate goods yard. In 1920 after we had moved to Aldershot, there was a coal strike and we came up and camped on Wimbledon Common. In the spring of 1921 there was another miners' strike and this time we went under canvas in Kensington Gardens. On this last occasion the situation was bad enough for Reservists to be called up for about two months.

Derek Murphy, self, Joe Ross, Edgar Maturin-Baird and Donald Hegerty at Chelsea, 1920

For the St Patrick's Day Parade in 1920 we went back into Full Dress uniform, the first time since 1914, and thereafter we returned to all the peacetime customs and uniforms, so perhaps it would be appropriate at this point to give some account of life in West End barracks at that period.

The day started for the men with Reveille at 6am. As soon as the bugle sounded, the Sergeants-in-waiting of each Company, who had to be already dressed, went round their Companies to ensure that everyone was out of bed and getting washed, shaved and dressed. Woe betide the man who was slow at getting out of bed and had the misfortune of having his bed near the door of the barrack room. The door would burst open and in would stride the Sergeant-in-waiting. Without a second thought he would pick up the bed of anyone still in it and turn it over sending the occupant flying.

The first parade at 6.30am was known as Breakfast Roll Call

36

and was taken by the Picquet Officer. It was held before breakfast in Fatigue Dress which consisted of brown canvas washable jacket and trousers (with detachable brass buttons) and khaki Service Dress caps. On one morning a week there was 'Blanket shaking' which meant that, working in pairs, the men shook their bed blankets and gave them a good airing. In those days, there were no sheets and no pyjamas, the men simply slept in their shirts. On other mornings, they were required to show some item of clothing or equipment, such as their spare pair of boots.

After breakfast there were Adjutant's Orders at 7.45am, and then at 8.45am Battalion Muster Parade conducted by the Adjutant and Regimental Sergeant Major, and all officers junior to the Adjutant would be required to attend. The battalion would parade in khaki Service Dress with forage caps (coloured peaked caps) and would fall in by drum tap. First the Adjutant would inspect all the Non-commissioned officers, and then the subalterns would inspect their platoons. After this there would be an hour's drill either by platoons or companies or sometimes the whole battalion would be drilled by the Regimental Sergeant Major, assisted by the Drill Sergeants. Young Officers would often be fallen in with the Corporals and drilled by one of the Drill Sergeants. Young Officers could have their names taken for being 'idle on parade' just as easily as the Corporals, and they would be punished by the Adjutant with Extra Picquets.

Tea break followed until 10.30am, and then there would be Company training, which might be musketry, physical training, etc. During this time, Company Orders would be held either by the Company Commanders who would have arrived in barracks by then or, if any were away as was very often the case, by the senior subaltern in each company. Young Officers were left in no doubt by the Company Sergeant Major as to what punishment was considered suitable for the various offenders. After hearing the evidence, one had only to ask: 'How does this man do, Sergeant Major?', to receive a very clear indication as to whether the man was to be let off with a warning or given a brisk punishment. I well remember one Company Sergeant Major who habitually made his views known in advance by addressing the culprit outside the Company Office in a loud voice which could be clearly heard by the officer inside: 'You know, Brown, what you're going to get, don't yer? Seven days CB.'

At 12 noon came the climax of the working day – Commanding Officer's Orders. This was conducted by the Drill Sergeant-in-waiting like a small scale Battalion Parade. The Sergeants-in-waiting and Corporals-in-waiting of each Company, accompanied by those men and indeed Non-commissioned officers of their Companies who had been remanded from Adjutant's Orders or Company Orders for offences or requests requiring the decision of higher authority, were fallen in by drum tap outside the Orderly Room just as on Battalion Parade. After the Company Commanders and other officers attending had entered the Orderly Room and ranged themselves behind the Commanding Officer and Adjutant who would be sitting side by side at the Orderly Room desk, the Regimental Sergeant Major would ask the Commanding Officer's leave to carry on with his Orders. Permission granted, the Drill Sergeant would wheel the men in and out at tremendous speed.

A delightful piece of etiquette ensured that Companies were summoned in order of the seniority of the Company Commander, so that the latter was able to salute and leave the Orderly Room as soon as his men had been 'dealt with', and the more senior officers would thus have time for an extra gin before lunch.

Men of equal rank were taken together, each taking a pace forward out of the ranks when his name was read out. After reading out the charge, witnesses were called. There was another delightful convention that, although present and able to intervene if necessary, officers did not give their own evidence. Thus the Corporal or Sergeant who had been ordered to take the man's name and place him in the Report, would start off: 'Mr Smith's report of 12th March. This man . . . etc' or if it had been the person taking Orders who had ordered the report, the NCO would start off: 'Your report of 15th June, Sir. This man . . . etc.' After hearing the evidence, the man would be asked if he had anything to say. His reply could be either: 'Nothing to say, Sir.' or 'Thank you for leave to speak, Sir. It was like this . . . etc.' Alas for the man who departed from this set form. Before he could get started with his excuse, the Sergeant Major would have thundered out: 'Thank the Officer for leave to speak!' Perhaps to modern ears this sounds rather high-handed, yet it had a steadying effect. Instead of blurting out a string of foolish excuses, the pause required to go through the set form gave a man time to pull himself together and think clearly what he was going to say. Punishment was now pronounced, and immediately the Sergeant Major would roar out: 'Fall In', whereupon the man took a pace back into the rank, and the next man was called out. As soon as all the men in the room had been 'weighed off', they were shot out and the next lot wheeled in.

Men in close arrest have to be seen by the Commanding Officer daily and they attend his Orders under escort. Sometimes such men are awaiting Court Martial and, knowing they have nothing to lose, refuse to behave. Instead of marching in smartly in step with the escort, they saunter out of step causing confusion to the escort who are terrified of 'losing their names' for being idle on escort duty. Instead of standing stiffly to attention while being asked if they have any complaints, they look around and even whistle under their breath. Needless to say, this almost causes apoplexy to the Sergeant Major! Sitting behind the Orderly Room desk, the Commanding Officer and Adjutant are rather vulnerable to assault by disgruntled miscreants as the escort seldom react quickly enough. I remember a man stepping out of the escort, picking up the edge of the Orderly Room desk, and overturning it on the unfortunate Commanding Officer and Adjutant who were not only thrown to the ground but also covered in ink!

I must not give the impression that Commanding Officer's Orders were concerned only with Crime and Punishment. There were many other reasons for being ordered to attend Commanding Officer's Orders such as men being promoted or sent on Training Courses outside the Regiment, men with family problems which could not be dealt with by their Company Commanders, and then there were men requesting permission to marry.

Both officers and men had to have the Commanding Officer's

permission to marry. The official minimum age was 30 for officers and 25 years of age for other ranks. While permission might in some circumstances be given to marry under the regulation age, the Army would not pay any Marriage Allowance in such cases. I need hardly say that if an officer proposed to marry a young lady who was considered socially unsuitable, he would be expected to resign his Commission. Guards Officers are members of the Court and therefore no scandal of any sort was allowed. So in those days, if an officer were involved in divorce proceedings, he would have to send in his papers.

Even to change his religion a man had to have Commanding Officer's permission as his religion was officially noted in his records. This reminds me of a story I heard about Sidney Fitz-Gerald when he was Commanding Officer. Apparently a man was marched in requesting permission to change his religion. As readers will have gathered, Black Fitz was renowned for his irascibility. After questioning the man who seemed very uncertain about the whole thing, Sidney exclaimed: 'It's not like changing your socks, you know!'

After the last lot had been seen, the Sergeant Major would conclude the proceedings by roaring out: 'That's all for your Orders, Sir' and the officers would adjourn to the Mess for luncheon.

If the Battalion was finding Public Duties that day, Duty-mounting would have taken place during the earlier part of the morning, conducted by the Adjutant and Regimental Sergeant Major. Duties comprising the two Detachments of the King's Guard, the Bank Picquet, the Hyde Park Magazine Guard and the Barrack Guard would be fallen in by drum tap; and the Adjutant would inspect first the Non-commissioned officers and then the men. When all was ready, he would hand the Duties over to the Captain of the Guard. The latter would fall in the Officers after which the Colour would be brought on parade from the Officers' Mess where it was kept and handed to the Ensign by the Regimental Sergeant Major. Duties would then march off, led by the Duty Band, and accompanied by the Drill Sergeant-out-of-waiting who would march in rear and keep an eagle eye open for any form of idleness. In those days there was no question of any transport, and duties marched either from Wellington Barracks or Chelsea irrespective of the weather. The ceremony of changing was carried out in the forecourt of Buckingham Palace only when the King was in residence, otherwise it was in Friary Court, St James's Palace.

The battalions in West End barracks had nothing to do with the Tower of London, which had its own garrison of a whole battalion in residence. The latter found no fewer than three separate Guards: the Main Guard on the Jewel House, the Spur Guard on the main entrance on Tower Hill, and the Wharf Guard under Tower Bridge which had the usual cells for men in arrest.

I was never stationed at Her Majesty's Royal Palace and Fortress of the Tower of London, to give it its full title, but I dined there with friends on a number of occasions. Although there were always plenty of sightseers, it was very much a fortress in those days and bristled with sentries. If the Commanding Officer wished to take the Battalion, other than the men on Guard, out on a route march or exercise, he had to obtain the written permission of the Resident Governor to remove the garrison. There had been 'Men at Arms' living in the Tower since it was built by William the Conqueror nine centuries ago, and to me it is sad that this tradition has finally been broken. Apart from a small ceremonial Guard, tourism now reigns supreme.

To return to our description of the daily routine in barracks, dinners were served in Company messes at 1pm and would be 'seen' by one of the Company officers. After the men had had a chance to sample the food, it was customary for the Sergeant-in-waiting to blow a whistle for silence, after which the Officer would say: 'Any complaints?' to which there would normally be a well-drilled chorus of 'No, sir!' On one occasion a newly-joined officer caused confusion by reversing the question and saying 'Dinner all right?' to which of course he received the routine reply of 'No, sir!' and then a few 'Yes, sirs' followed after a slight hesitation by an outraged bellow from the Sergeant-in-waiting: 'Wake up, you dozy men, answer the Officer properly!'

41

Spring Drills in preparation for the King's Birthday Parade would sometimes be held in the afternoon; but for most of the year while in garrison, there would be no parades after dinner and the men were free to walk out from 1.30pm. Young soldiers with less than one year's service had to attend the 1.30pm Drill Parade conducted by the Picquet Officer and Drill Sergeant-in-waiting; but as soon as they 'passed out' on this parade, they were excused it.

At 3.30pm there was Punishment Parade for Defaulters also taken by the Picquet Officer and Drill Sergeant-in-waiting. Although the Picquet Officer had to attend the forming-up of these parades and inspect the men; he would then tell the Drill Sergeant to carry on, and the latter would give an hour's drill to the men down for Extra Drills and those undergoing CB punishment.

In view of the astronomic cost of scarlet tunics these days, readers will be astonished to learn that, although the soldiers were issued with their first 'best' tunic and trousers and also with all their khaki Service Dress uniform and equipment, they were given a Clothing Allowance out of which they had to maintain their tunics and underwear and also buy for themselves a 'second tunic'. Soldiers were engaged for twelve years, either seven with the Colours and five with the Reserve or four with the Colours and eight with the Reserve. The majority took the latter option so there were always plenty of men going on Reserve who held Kit sales at which 'Second tunics' could be bought.

'Best' tunics were kept for Guard and 'Second tunics' for walking out and for sentry on Guard at night. Men walking out were forbidden to lie on the grass in the Royal Parks; but they had every incentive to look after their tunics as they had to pay for their replacement.

Walking Out Dress was Second tunic, white buff waistbelt, coloured forage cap and cane. Many people think of swagger canes being peculiar to officers; but this is not the case at all. Until 1939, the British Army had been unique in that all ranks always carried a swagger cane off duty. In mounted units a whip was carried in place of a cane; and there was a complete section in the Drill Book for drill with cane or whip. No doubt carrying a cane added greatly to the smartness of the soldiers off duty and of course they were much less inclined to place their hands in their pockets if they had something to hold.

Blue patrol jackets for walking out did not come in until after the Second War and Mess Kit for senior NCOs not until the late fifties.

To post-war generations, who have never seen soldiers or sailors in uniform except on duty, there can be no idea of the scene in pre-war London or indeed in any of the great cities or garrison towns. In London alone there were five battalions of Footguards, two regiments of Household Cavalry, and a battery of the Royal Horse Artillery, all of whom were released onto the streets in uniform at 1.30pm daily. The happy hunting grounds were the Royal Parks where, as we know from Christopher Robin, the Guardsmen were wont to meet pretty nursemaids, who were walking their charges in perambulators. Tea was available back in barracks but to many men 'square-pushing' provided a more sociable and far better meal. The great houses of Mayfair and Belgravia were mostly ranged round large leafy squares – hence the expression 'square-pushing'. All had large staffs with cook reigning supreme in the basement. The trades-men's entrance was down the outside steps into the area outside the large kitchen. Cooks were happy to feed a handsome Guardsman and he might even get a glass of port from the butler. Any mistress who dared to come unexpectedly into cook's domain, might well find a couple of Guardsmen eating her food and maybe also the local policeman, who would himself probably be a Guards reservist. Soldiers with really good con-tacts, who found themselves confined to barracks, might be fortunate enough to have 'square-pushing through the railings': that is their cook would bring some choice morsels and pass them through the barrack railings after dark.

Officers' servants and very senior Non-commissioned officers had permission to wear plain clothes, but for the remainder plain clothes could only be worn at home on long leave. They even had to travel to and from home in uniform. Officers' servants wore pin-striped trousers and black jackets with bowler hats like valets, their civilian counterparts.

43

Most of the men had Midnight Passes, but a minor punishment was the loss of this Pass which meant that the man had to be back in barracks by 10pm. At First Post (9.30pm) the Drill Sergeant-in-waiting paraded all the Sergeants-in-waiting and the latter went round their Companies checking that all defaulters and men 'On the gate' were present in their barrack rooms. At Last Post (10pm) the Barrack Guard turned out and all Defaulters had to parade with the Guard. The Sergeants-in-waiting reported to the Drill Sergeant who in turn reported to the Picquet Officer. The latter inspected the Defaulters and then dismissed them, and they had 15 minutes to be in bed before 'Lights Out'. All the defaulters and men 'Confined to Barracks' were on a List held in the Guardroom. As each man left barracks he had to report to the Sergeant or Corporal of the Guard who not only checked that he was properly dressed but that he was not on the List – hence the expression being 'On the gate'.

Officers wore Full Dress tunics and bearskins for Guard and other Ceremonial Parades; but otherwise wore frogged Frock coats with blue gold-braided forage caps – a very smart uniform indeed. This was worn in barracks by the Adjutant, Picquet Officer, and indeed all the junior officers; and when one went into the Mess for luncheon one removed the frock coat and replaced it with a blue 'jumper' or patrol jacket. In London the Commanding Officer and senior officers would wear plain clothes in barracks but at Windsor or Aldershot khaki Service Dress was usually worn.

Mess Kit was worn for dinner except at weekends when plain clothes could be worn; but in London there was hardly ever anyone dining except the Picquet Officer. At Windsor or Aldershot it was more usual for officers to dine in Mess and there would be occasional Guest Nights at which guests who were not soldiers would wear white tie and tails.

Occasionally the King would give a State Ball at Buckingham Palace in honour of some visiting Royalty, and each regiment in the London garrison had to produce a quota of officers who attended in Full Dress uniform. Bearskin caps and greatcoats would be left in the cloakroom; but swords had to be worn at the

Ball except when actually dancing!

For work on the ranges or on Autumn Manoeuvres, officers wore khaki Service Dress uniform with khaki peaked caps and blackthorn sticks. In those days puttees were still worn not only by the men but also by officers unless they were mounted in which case they wore breeches and boots.

In London in those far off days, morning dress and silk top hats were worn for far more functions than they are now; but even if formal clothes were not worn, officers had to be dressed in lounge suits and bowler hats; and the standard penalty for being seen in London without a hat was seven days Extra Picquets. In the evening, the normal dress was white tie and tails, dinner jackets being only worn when dining at home *en famille*.

From this it can be seen that except when sent down to the ranges or on manoeuvres duties were not too onerous for either officers or men. The principal chore in garrison was King's Guard; but with four battalions in the West End the battalion only had to find the Guard every four days, so this duty did not come round too frequently. The Captain of the Guard was normally either a Captain or a Major, though on special occasions it could be taken by the Commanding Officer himself. There were two Subalterns, one each for the St James's and Buckingham Palace Detachments, and an Ensign to carry the Colour. There was little time to be bored on Guard as we entertained extensively. Hardly had we completed the Guard-mounting ceremony and changed into our blue jumpers than guests arrived for drinks before luncheon. Some guests, including ladies, remained to lunch with us and others might come to tea. Soon after our earlier guests left, we changed into Mess Kit in time to receive our dinner guests who would be gentlemen only.

Our busiest time was the summer, starting with Spring Drills to prepare ourselves for all the ceremonial duties of the London Season culminating in the King's Birthday Parade or Trooping of the Colour as it is commonly called. After the Season was over there was a short break before Autumn Manoeuvres; and then we came to the 'Leave Season' from October to March.

For Public Duties there had to be a captain or major and five subalterns or ensigns – three for King's Guard, one for the Bank Picquet and one for Picquet Officer in barracks. It was therefore necessary to have at least two Company Commanders and about a dozen young officers not on leave at any one time. This meant that senior officers and even the senior subalterns could expect about three or four months leave during the Leave Season while even the ensigns and junior subalterns would get six to eight weeks. By modern standards this must seem astonishing but we thought nothing of it, as we were living in an age when it was not considered compulsory to work for one's living and there were still many gentlemen of independent means who did nothing at all except devise means of enjoying themselves.

Even in summer, it was not difficult to get leave for sporting activities, especially polo which did indeed improve one's horsemanship. At such times as Ascot Week, one would not find a soul in barracks other than the unfortunate chap who had been landed for Picquet Duty. It was the duty of the Senior Subaltern to draw up the Duty List and he had the privilege of omitting his own name from the List. Apart from the regular roster for this duty, there were frequently miscreants who had fallen foul of the Adjutant and been punished with Extra Picquets. Although this was hard on the poor chap concerned, it was very good news for the remaining subalterns as they were relieved of the duty. As we shall see, I had the misfortune of having more than my fair share of Extra Picquets!

My parents took a house at 38 Park Lane in 1919 where they remained until my mother's death in 1925. I naturally came home a good deal while stationed at Chelsea and my half-sister, Claire, who was then 19, was doing the social round of parties and balls. We tended to lead our own lives and I fear that I did not bring her into my own social life very much, though she was great friends with two of my brother officers, Guy and George Repton, whose parents lived in nearby Curzon Street. Then in December 1920, she married Roy Stewart and had a splendid society wedding at the Brompton Oratory.

At about this time, Warwick had an ocean-going yacht called the *Suzanne* which won one of the principal events at Cowes. I

My sister, Claire

was with Warwick on that triumphant occasion and I remember having to uncover and bow as we sailed past King George V who was standing on the deck of a warship.

Warwick, who was always keen on new gadgets and ideas, gave me a motor scooter which he had imported from America. It must have been ahead of its time as it did not catch on; and it was not until after the Second War that motor scooters became popular. However, it was something of a novelty at the time and aroused considerable interest. My Company Commander, Reggie Sassoon, bet me £50 to £1 that I would not ride it in uniform past the sentries on King's Guard when the Regiment was on duty. I did so, wearing my Frock Undress uniform, and won the bet; but I did it very early in the morning when nobody was about. The astonished sentries duly saluted me and I did not

Warwick's yacht, Suzanne

48

get caught by the Adjutant or any senior officer so all was well. I had a great admiration for Reggie, who besides being ready to take on any sort of bet or gamble, had tremendous courage. Despite very poor sight, he decided to ride in the Grand National Steeplechase at Aintree and, although he came in last, he was so much admired that all the professional jockeys lined up at the finish to cheer him in.

Soon after we moved to Chelsea Jim Keenan rejoined the Battalion. Jim had been to Downside before the War and went up to Trinity College, Cambridge, in 1914; but after only one term he was commissioned into the Regiment early in 1915. He went out to France with the 2nd Battalion and was wounded twice. After recovering he was posted to the 1st Battalion as Adjutant and was wounded a third time. He had been in hospital for nearly a year so I had not met him before. We became great friends and used to go around a good deal with Claire and the Repton brothers.

Tom Vesey, who had been my Commanding Officer when I joined the Reserve Battalion at Warley in 1917, was now commanding the 1st Battalion, and in the spring of 1920, Alex returned to us from the Baltic and became Second-in-Command, reverting to Major to do so.

The Regimental Sergeant Major at this time was Tom Cahill, who was later to go to Downside as Sergeant Major of the Officers' Training Corps. Tom was one of the earliest recruits, having joined the Regiment in 1901, and he became Regimental Sergeant Major of the 1st Battalion in 1916, a post he held until his retirement from the Army in 1922. He was Mentioned in Despatches three times and won the Distinguished Conduct Medal in France. After retiring from the Army he went to Downside and became an institution, known to generations of Downside boys between the Wars. He also joined the King's Bodyguard of the Yeoman of the Guard, for which he used to grow an Imperial beard, and would disappear to London from time to time for such events as the State Opening of Parliament.

In the summer of 1921, we moved to Victoria Barracks, Windsor, which was a delightful station, with every sort of recreational and sporting facility available to us. It was rather

Tom Cahill, c 1920

fun mounting Castle Guard, as there was only one officer who occupied the Officer's Guardroom over the main Castle gateway, which comprised one quite large room with a curtained recess for a bed. Here we were allowed to entertain young ladies to luncheon or tea and gentlemen to dinner.

One of my young friends from the school serving in the Regiment very kindly invited me to dine on Guard with him when the Regiment was stationed there quite recently. It must have been sixty years since I had last been in that fascinating room. It is the custom for officers to carve their initials and sometimes their regimental emblems on the wooden walls of the bed cubicle. Rather like the prisoners in the Tower of London, generations of officers over more than one hundred years have relieved the tedium of their duty by carving their initials and even poems on the walls. I would like to be able to say that we found my own initials; but we searched in vain, so perhaps I never bothered.

One very hot day when Jim Keenan was Officer of the Guard, he had removed his tunic and was relaxing in his shirtsleeves, when the Corporal of the Guard came running up the stairs and said: 'Oh sir, the Queen wants to see you! She's downstairs with Princess Mary and she wants to know if she can come up'. 'Oh yes' says Jim, hastily putting on his tunic and cummerbund. The Queen and Princess then came up to view a crayon drawing over the mantelpiece which the King had recently had covered with glass to preserve it. They stayed chatting for some time and had tea with him.

It was then and still is the rather pleasant custom for the Monarch to invite the Officer of the Guard to dinner from time to time when the Court is in residence at Windsor. I never had this honour, perhaps because I was posted to Extra-Regimental Duty very soon after we had arrived at Windsor.

In the autumn Francis Law was appointed ADC to Field Marshal Viscount Plumer GCB GCMG GCVO, who was then Governor and Commander-in-Chief of Malta, and he sailed with Lord Plumer when the latter returned from leave. Malta was to be granted self-government and the Prince of Wales was to represent the King at the Opening of their first Parliament.

The ceremonies were timed to take place as the Prince sailed to India in *HMS Renown*. It was then decided that an additional ADC was required to assist with all the extra work entailed by the Prince's visit. I was detailed to join Francis out there, and this proved to be one of the happiest times of my life.

Chapter 4

Malta

No one sailing into Grand Harbour, Valetta, for the first time can fail to be tremendously impressed by the sheer size of the harbour and the towering battlements of the fortresses built by the Knights of Malta to repel the Turkish invaders – not to mention the might of the serried ranks of battleships and cruisers lying at anchor which in those days comprised the Mediterranean Fleet. Valetta is in fact one of the two largest natural harbours in the whole Mediterranean, the other being Port Mahon at Minorca.

The Knights are so much part of the history of Malta and I have been so involved in the affairs of the Island that I think I should say a brief word about them.

The Sovereign Military Hospitaller Order of St John of Jerusalem has its origins in the Crusades and is the oldest Order of Chivalry still in existence. Even before the Crusades there were pilgrims to the Holy Land who were tolerated by the Moslems. About 1080 some merchants of Amalfi who transported pilgrims from their port to the Holy Land established a Hospice for pilgrims in Jerusalem. Following the First Crusade and the capture of Jerusalem in 1099 this Hospice was greatly enlarged and received generous grants of land from Godfrey of Bouillon and Baldwin of Boulogne, the first two rulers of the Christian Kingdom of Jerusalem, who took the Hospital under their care and protection. This example was followed by many other European rulers and Hospitals were soon operated by the Order at all the main pilgrim embarkation ports such as Marseilles, Bari and Messina. Meanwhile the necessity of protecting

Christians from the Moslems on the pilgrim routes led to the foundation of the other great Military Orders, such as the Knights Templar. The Order of St John followed suit, establishing a chain of fortresses in Palestine and providing pilgrims with both food and rest, nursing facilities, and military protection. The brothers who worked in the Hospitals were both priests and laymen; but all took strict vows of poverty, chastity and obedience. Later, noble birth became a *sine qua non* for membership, though all had to take the vows.

After the fall of Acre in 1291 when the Christians were finally driven out of Palestine, the Order was without a home until 1307 when it took the Island of Rhodes which it held for two centuries and where the Hospital was re-established. The Order now became a naval as well as a military power, policing the Mediterranean against Saracen pirates which plagued it down to Napoleonic times. It also constituted a bulwark against Turkish attack on Europe, and was a permanent thorn in the side of the Moslems.

After an unsuccessful siege in 1480, the Turks under the Sultan Suleiman the Magnificent again laid siege to the Island in 1522 and this time after six months the Knights finally surrendered with honour. Among the survivors was a young knight called Jean de la Valette. Once more they were without a home, but in 1530 the Knights were given Malta by the Emperor Charles V of Spain.

Jean de la Valette became Grand Master in 1557 and in 1565 the Sultan Suleiman, who had defeated the Knights at Rhodes in his youth, forty three years earlier, returned to the attack. The Great Siege of Malta lasted from May until September and was unsuccessful. La Valette had held out with 9,000 men against 40,000 Turks; but at the end he had only 600 men left and some 250 Knights had been killed. It was a great victory for Christendom. Had Malta been lost, there is no doubt Suleiman intended to invade Europe having secured the Mediterranean. This was well appreciated by European rulers – including our own Protestant Queen Elizabeth – and funds came flowing in with which to build and fortify the new city of Valetta named after the great Grand Master who was the first to be buried within its walls.

Valetta is a beautiful city with its outstanding buildings such as the Conventual Church of St John the Baptist, now the Co-cathedral, and the great Hospital of the Order. In addition there are the Auberges (Inns) of the various Langues or Tongues and many private residences of Knights. The Order was organised into eight national groups called Langues: three French, two Spanish, and the Italian, German and English. The latter had been suppressed by Henry VIII at the time of the Reformation, though La Valette's Latin Secretary was an Englishman, Sir Oliver Starkey, who composed the following epitaph which is inscribed in Latin on the Grand Master's tomb in the crypt of the Conventual Church: 'Here lies La Valette, worthy of eternal honour, he who was formerly the terror of Asia and Africa and the shield of Europe, whence by his holy arms he expelled the barbarians, the first to be buried in the beloved city of which he was the founder.'

Although the fortifications were enlarged and strengthened there were no further attacks until Napoleon came with his Fleet *en route* for Egypt in 1798. By then the Order had decayed to such an extent that scarcely a shot was fired, and the Knights were expelled ignominiously from the Island.

It remains a Sovereign Order with its Headquarters in Rome at the Palazzo di Malta; but it has returned to its original objects: the relief of the poor and the sick. There are now some 8,000 Knights throughout the world but most are married, only a few, of whom two are English, being fully professed and taking the full vows. Priests can become Chaplains to the Order and, as we shall see, I later had the honour to be made one.

Soon after my arrival, numerous VIPs started to arrive to take part in the self-government celebrations, including Colonel Lionel Amery representing the British Government. There were a succession of ceremonies before the Prince of Wales' arrival in which first the Senate and then the Legislative Assembly were sworn in, culminating in a great Pontifical High Mass of the Holy Spirit in St John's Cathedral in Valetta to seek the blessing of Almighty God on the new Parliament.

Mr Joseph Howard was the first Prime Minister and Mr Arrigo was the Speaker, while Sir Gerald Strickland (later Lord

Strickland) led the Opposition. However, apart from the Governor, the most important person on the Island in those days was undoubtedly the Archbishop, Maurus Caruana. He ranked as a Major General and the Guard turned out and presented arms to him when he called on the Governor. His car and the Governor's were the only two on the Island with no number plates: his simply had a Mitre painted on it and the Governor's had a Crown. He was Maltese but had been educated in Scotland by the Benedictines of Fort Augustus Abbey and on leaving the school had entered the monastery there. From being a simple monk, he had been appointed Bishop of Malta and later received the honorary rank of Archbishop. As ADC to the Governor, I saw both him and his Secretary, Monsignor Michael Gonzi, on many occasions. They were to have a considerable influence upon me and were at least in part responsible for my later vocation to the priesthood.

On All Saints' Day, 1st November, the great battle cruiser *HMS Renown* and her escorts arrived in Grand Harbour, to the sound of a nineteen gun salute, and Lord Plumer accompanied by Francis Law went aboard to welcome the Prince. They then returned ashore and Francis went to the Palace to see that all was ready, while I remained with Lord Plumer at the Custom House quay to receive His Royal Highness as he came ashore with his entourage. The Prince, wearing naval uniform and accompanied by his ADC, Lord Louis Mountbatten (later Earl Mountbatten of Burma) and other members of his staff, proceeded to the Castille Palace in Valetta where he stood on a dais in the Ballroom and declared the new Parliament open. Francis and I then had to marshal a vast concourse of officials and legislators to be presented to him in proper order of precedence. This was eventually followed by luncheon in the Prince's honour at the Casino Maltese.

After luncheon we rushed back to the San Anton Palace to ensure that all was ready for the Garden Party. In the evening there was an official dinner at the Palace followed by a great Ball. The following day the Prince visited the Cathedral in Mdina and then attended an informal luncheon at Admiralty House. In the afternoon there was a gymkhana at the Marsa

At the dockyard: The Prince, Lord Plumer, unknown, Colonel Samut (Dom Denis Agius' grandfather), myself and Francis Law

racecourse and the Prince was wheeled in a barrow race by his brother, Prince George, who was then a Midshipman in the flagship, causing a sensation among the Maltese spectators!

In the evening the Prince attended a performance in the delightful little Opera House in Valetta. I was in the Royal Box and I could not help noticing how intensely bored he was with the opera. It was definitely not his type of fun. The Opera House, which was destroyed in the Second War and has never been replaced, had been built in mid-Victorian times to the design of the same architect as Covent Garden. Before it was built, the Manoel Theatre, a little gem built by the Knights as a miniscule copy of La Scala at Milan, had been used as Valetta's Opera House. After the War it was restored to its original use and is said to be the oldest theatre in Europe. Only the boxes on one side of the auditorium were for the public, those on the other side being owned on long leases by members of the Maltese nobility.

After yet another dinner at the Palace, we drove down to Grand Harbour to take leave of His Royal Highness as he returned to the *Renown* and sailed away the next morning to the sound of the customary gun salutes.

In addition to attending on the Governor at military parades and inspections, the ADCs had the job of arranging the seating in strict order of precedence and issuing the invitations to the many luncheons and dinners given by His Excellency, so after the Royal visit Francis and I were pretty exhausted. However, even in the normal way there were several such functions each week which we attended ourselves and we also accompanied the Governor to return dinners with the Naval C-in-C, the Archbishop, the Lieutenant Governor, the Military Commander, etc.

I got on very well with 'Plum' as we always called the Governor and even more importantly I got on well with Lady Plumer who had a reputation for being 'difficult'. Francis disliked her intensely and early in the New Year applied to return to duty with the Regiment, leaving me as the permanent ADC in his place.

In April 1922, Alex succeeded Colonel Tom Vesey in command of the 1st Battalion at Windsor and Sidney FitzGerald became Adjutant. Soon afterwards the Battalion sailed for Constantinople as part of a peace-keeping force. Owing to a shortage of officers, I was sent on temporary loan to form part of the Advance Party and I sailed direct from Malta in a destroyer, leaving a Maltese officer to look after 'Plum' in my absence. The ship's officers had celebrated their departure the night before not wisely but too well, and to my amazement the ship was taken to sea by a Midshipman. I became very good friends with him on the voyage and little did we know then that he was to become Vice Admiral Sir Ballin Robertshaw KBE CB. Many years later during the Second War he got me a passage to North Africa in a battleship, having by that time become a Captain. We met again in Malta after the War, by which time he had become an Admiral.

The Battalion arrived in the Golden Horn on 12th May and were greeted by the Allied Commander-in-Chief, General Sir Charles Harington GCB GBE DSO, who had been Chief of Staff to Lord Plumer when the latter was commanding the 2nd Army in France. Although his Christian name was Charles, for some reason he was always known as 'General Tim'. The troops disembarked and, led by Colonel Alex and the Colour Party, marched through the city with fixed bayonets to Tash Kishla barracks on the outskirts overlooking the Bosphorus. The Officers' Mess had a long verandah overlooking the waterway with a splendid view of Scutari on the other side, where Florence Nightingale had had her hospital during the Crimean War.

I was of course very pleased to be once more with many of my friends like Jim Keenan, Edgar Maturin-Baird and Derek Murphy. Derek always had a hot temper and one day got very cross playing tennis with Kenneth Hogg, his Company Commander. Finally, he threw down his racket, exclaiming: 'I will take your orders, but I shall not speak to you ever again!' This lasted about one day!

I met Jim Keenan recently and he reminded me how we used to go with the Repton brothers across the Golden Horn into the old city to the Turkish Baths.

I spent several months in Constantinople before returning to Malta and found it a fascinating city. One episode which comes to mind was when I went with Colonel Alex soon after our arrival to pay an official call upon the Sultan, the last of a long line of Ottoman rulers which had lasted 500 years. He abdicated the following November, was smuggled out of his Palace in an ambulance and sailed in *HMS Malaya* to Malta where I was in attendance when the Governor received him. He had a large retinue and was housed in a barracks which luckily was empty at the time. He was an embarrassment to the British Government; but fortunately the French offered to take him off our hands.

While in Constantinople I was lucky enough to be shown round the Sultan's Seraglio, the women's quarters of his Palace. It had a bloody history, having been the scene of the massacre of the Janisseries, the Sultan's Bodyguard. This Guard had been founded in the 14th century and lasted until the early part of the 19th century when it was thought to have become too powerful and was treacherously slaughtered to a man on the then Sultan's orders. We were also shown an 'oubliette' in the Palace walls where numerous wretches must have been murdered down the centuries. A strong current flows down the Bosphorus into the Sea of Marmara round Seraglio Point on which the Palace stands, and an underground passage had been built diverting part of the stream under the walls of the Palace. The 'oubliette' was a hole with a sheer drop which enabled victims trussed in a sack to be dropped into the underground stream, washed out to sea and drowned.

On another occasion I went with Colonel Alex and some other officers to the mosque of Santa Sophia to witness a service from the gallery in the dome. We looked down from a great height onto the praying figures far below. It was formerly a great Christian cathedral dating from the time of Justinian and could hold seven thousand of the faithful.

I have good reason to be thankful to Edgar Baird. One day I was in charge of a bathing party which I took for a swim in the Bosphorus. As I have mentioned, there is a strong current and one man was swept away and brought out apparently drowned. Fortunately, Edgar happened to be with me and he applied artificial respiration and succeeded in reviving the man.

Just before I left, we celebrated the King's Birthday by Trooping the Colour with the Buffs on the Taxime Parade Ground before General Tim and our Ambassador. It created quite an impression on the Turks.

After my return to Malta I settled down to the routine of a Governor's ADC, which I found much to my liking.

In those days there was a very considerable garrison of some three battalions of infantry, a number of Coastal Defence batteries of the Royal Garrison Artillery, three Regiments of the Royal Malta Artillery, a Fortress Company of the Sappers plus attached RASC. In addition there was the Royal Malta Light Infantry, a Territorial unit. The Gordon Highlanders were on the Island during the whole of my tour. When I first arrived there were also the Essex and the Royal Sussex Regiments, but later these were relieved by the Dorset and East Lancashire Regiments. Although the Governor was Commander-in-Chief, there was also a General Officer Commanding the Troops.

On the naval side, there was the Commander-in-Chief, Mediterranean Fleet, Sir John de Roebeck, who resided in Admiralty House at Valetta, when not flying his Flag in the battleship *Iron Duke*. Admiralty House had formerly been the private residence of one of the Knights of Malta. He had his Shore Office in the Auberge of Castille which also housed the

ADC to Lord Plumer, Malta 1921

Headquarters of the GOC and had a naval Signal Station on the roof. I am told that this historic building is now used as the Office of the Prime Minister and his Staff. Sir John was later replaced by Admiral Sir Osmond de Beauvoir Brock.

Besides Sir John, there were a number of junior admirals commanding various squadrons, not to mention that important personage, Rear Admiral Luce, the Admiral Superintendent of the Dockyard. Rear Admiral Sir Richard Webb had his Flag in *Benbow* commanding the 4th Battle Squadron, the other battle-ships being *King George V, Emperor of India* and *Centurion.* Then there was the 3rd Light Cruiser Squadron commanded by Rear Admiral Sir Reginald Tyrwhitt, later to become an Admiral of the Fleet. There was also a flotilla of destroyers which were berthed in Sliema Creek.

On the civil side, there were the Lieutenant Governor and the Chief Secretary, both Colonial Service officers.

All in all, there were a large number of VIPs to entertain and to be entertained by; and I came to know them very well.

Our little Court wintered in the Palace in Valetta, a very impressive building of great historic interest, having been built by the famous fighting Grand Master La Valette soon after the Great Siege. We spent spring and autumn at San Anton about half way along the road between Valetta and Mdina, and the hot summer months at the delightful Verdala Palace. Malta is a very barren rocky island with little vegetation but the Verdala Palace, built like the others by the Knights, is situated on the only part of the island which was wooded and in which the Knights used to go hunting.

For small dinner parties I wore my ordinary Regimental Mess Dress but for large evening parties at the Palace I had a special uniform consisting of the usual white tie, stiff shirt, waistcoat and a tail coat with pale blue ribbed silk facings and lining – very smart indeed. At these frequent dinner parties I came to know my opposite numbers, the other ADCs, the Flag Lieutenants of the various admirals, and above all Michael Gonzi, the Arch-bishop's Secretary. When I returned to the Island many years later, he had become Archbishop himself and our earlier friend-ship proved very important.

I came to meet some of the Maltese nobility including the Baroness Inguanez whose home, the Casa Inguanez at Mdina, was the oldest on the island, dating back to 1350. Her husband, Colonel MacKeen, had once commanded the Inniskilling Dragoons and the great cavalry leader, Lord Allenby, had been one of his subalterns.

I also met Sir Gerald Strickland's large family, including his famous daughter, Mabel, who later ran *The Times of Malta.* Sir Gerald, who received a United Kingdom peerage in 1928, was also a member of the Maltese nobility, being the 6th Count della Catena, a title dating back to 1745. However, my real pal for dances and parties was one of his younger daughters, Henrietta. We were never in love but we went around together a lot; and she confided in me that she intended to become a nun. It is perhaps ironic that it was I, at that time having no intention of doing so, who became a monk. Far from becoming a nun, she soon afterwards married Bob Bower, the C-in-C's Flag Lieutenant, and had eight children. However, she was undoubtedly very religious and after the Second War she started 'All Night Vigil' prayer groups and promoted many pilgrimages to Lourdes.

Her husband was a very colourful character who was at one time light heavy weight boxing champion of the Navy. He had been in submarines during the First War and was in convoys during the Second. Afterwards he entered Parliament and on one occasion told Mr Emmanuel Shinwell rather uncharitably to go back to Poland. Shinwell riposted by crossing the floor of the House and hitting him so hard that his eardrum was burst and he was deaf for the rest of his life. It must be recorded that on his 90th birthday Shinwell said that the one thing he regretted was hitting Commander Bower. Bob was too old to come back from Malta for the party but he spoke on Malta TV and said it was entirely his fault. So all was forgiven!

I was very inexperienced and must have been rather a trial to 'Plum' at first; but he tolerated me because I got on so well with 'Lady Plum', and I also think he was glad to have a Catholic ADC in so Catholic a country. However, I quickly got to know the ropes and later I think he came to look upon me as a son. It was a marvellous experience which has stood me in good stead throughout my life. As ADC, I lived with the family and, as I have said, had to work closely with 'Lady Plum' in arranging the seating at parties while observing the strict rules of precedence.

That reminds me of the races at Marsa. There was of course a Governor's Box and one of my jobs on race days was to usher the various VIPs into the Box and out again to make way for others at each race. For instance, I might have to get the Lieutenant Governor and his lady into the Box for the first race, the Naval C-in-C for the second, the GOC Troops for the third, and so on. Quite a feat of speed and tact!

'Plum' was very autocratic. He hated tobacco and would not tolerate smoking anywhere near him. He would not allow smoking at dinner parties at the Palaces even after the ladies had withdrawn and left the men with their port. On one occasion we were visited by the Queen of Rumania who was quite a character and clearly a forerunner of 'women's lib'. After a dinner given in her honour, she demanded a cigarette and when it was not forthcoming reached under her skirt and brought out a packet of cigarettes and a box of matches which she evidently kept in the top of her stocking. She then proceeded to light up much to 'Plum's' fury and mortification!

Malta has a marvellous climate and catered for every kind of sport. There were tennis, swimming, sailing, polo and squash. I played a lot of the latter as I reckoned that one obtained the maximum exercise in the minimum time.

Eventually, 'Plum's' tour of duty came to an end and in May 1924, we returned to England; but, as we shall see, I was destined to return to my beloved Malta many years later in a very different capacity.

Chapter 5

Vocation

After taking leave of Lord Plumer and going on leave myself, I reported back for duty with the Battalion which had meanwhile returned from Turkey and was now stationed at Inkerman Barracks, Woking.

I was of course pleased to be back with all my old friends in the Regiment. My hero, Colonel Alex, was still in command, Francis Law, Jim Keenan, Eddie FitzClarence and Derek Murphy were all there; and shortly afterwards Edgar Maturin-Baird rejoined us from the Depot. Sidney FitzGerald was still Adjutant and I was about to have several brushes with him in his official capacity.

In July 1924, we returned to London and Public Duties. I was with one half of the Battalion in Hyde Park Barracks and the other half was at Wellington Barracks. I cannot recall why we were split up or indeed why as Footguards we should have been occupying one of the Cavalry barracks. However, it was only for a short spell and in October we all moved to Chelsea.

Soon after we arrived at Knightsbridge, Charles Haydon, one of my fellow subalterns, brought a young guest called Claude van Zeller into the Mess. I little realised that Claude was to become Dom Hubert van Zeller. He had been in the school at Downside and was about to return there as a postulant and was 'clothed' in September 1924, just a year before me; but he did not reveal this at the time. Hubert, who became a great friend when I came to know him later in the monastery, was a very talented artist, sculptor and cartoonist and is famous for the series of humorous books he has written about monks and nuns, including *Cracks in the Cloisters*, as well as many devotional works.

It was at about this time that Joe Vandeleur joined us. He was later to command the 32nd Guards Armoured Brigade and to lead the attack in relief of the Arnhem landings. This action was portrayed in the film *A Bridge Too Far* and Michael Caine took the part of Brigadier Joe. He really was a hero to the Guardsmen, many of whom had his photograph as a 'pin-up' over their bunks. Joe never had much time for ceremonial and much preferred active duty. After quite a short time 'square-bashing', he got fed up and had the temerity to march himself into the Adjutant and request a transfer to the Seaforth Highlanders. Fortunately for the Regiment, Black Fitz was not having any of that and Joe went on to become a great Mick. However, a year or two later he did succeed in getting himself seconded to the Camel Corps in the Sudan.

Another colourful character I recall from those days was 'Flash' Kellett – I cannot remember his Christian name: but his nickname exactly describes him! He was a great gambler and always wanted to go over to Le Touquet at weekends to play the tables. If he were detailed as Picquet Officer on a Saturday or Sunday, he would offer his fellow subalterns a fiver, which was then a considerable sum, to take his duty for him.

This reminds me of the problem I had about attending Mass when detailed for King's Guard on a Saturday. Sundays presented no problem, as I could get up early and go to Mass before breakfast and then parade for Guard about 9.30am; but in those days Mass was not permitted to start after midday, so there was no question of going to an evening Mass. Fortunately the time for Guard-mounting was then 10.30am so we normally got back to barracks at about 11.45am. This did not allow much time for getting to church and certainly not for changing out of uniform. I therefore used to order a taxi to be standing waiting for me at the side of the Parade Ground and the moment the Officers had been fallen out, I would leap into the taxi in my Full Dress uniform and drive to Farm Street where I would stand at the back of the church carrying my bearskin under my arm. I suppose my appearance must have caused quite a stir and on one occasion I had great trouble with an officious verger who tried to get me to come forward into one of the pews, not realising that the uniform was so tight that it was almost impossible to sit down, let alone kneel!

One of the Public Duties which we carried out was the Bank Picquet which was only discontinued as recently as 1973 after nearly 200 years. It was originally provided to protect the Bank after the Gordon Riots in 1780, and was a very popular duty with both officers and men. The Bank had not then been nationalised and it paid a special bounty according to rank to every man of the Picquet. The Officer, who was normally a subaltern, had his own quarters and was served an excellent dinner at the Bank's expense in his private room, to which he was permitted to invite a gentleman friend.

The Picquet marched down to the City from the West End barracks every evening at 6pm and dismounted and returned to barracks at 6am the following morning. In those days of cheap fares it was quite customary for the officer to decide to pay for the Picquet to travel by train from Sloane Square Station to the Mansion House to avoid the fatigue of marching the whole way; and this was normally permitted. However, in order to help recruiting, an order was issued that the Bank Picquet should for the time being march all the way through the streets to the City and back each day, without the option of taking the tube. I accepted this edict and marched down to the Bank when I was on duty; but it seemed to me pointless to march back next morning through the empty streets, so I decided to bring the Picquet back by train. Unfortunately for me, as we marched back into barracks and dismissed, Sidney FitzGerald, the Adjutant, was shaving and looking out of his window he saw us. A glance at his watch and a quick calculation told him that we could not have got back so early if we had marched, so I was 'booked' and duly given seven days Extra Picquets, which in effect meant being confined to barracks.

Although I had very much enjoyed my time in Malta as ADC, promotion was extremely slow and I was still only a Lieutenant after nearly ten years service. I felt there was no real future in the Army and my thoughts turned to leaving and following in

Warwick's footsteps as a politician. I decided to go to a school for speech-training where I was given sample political speeches with which to practise. When I read the usual dreary platitudes which make up so many political speeches, I quickly realised that I had no real interest in politics and that this was not a life I should enjoy.

I suppose that I was more devout than the average young officer, and for many years I had tried to get to Mass daily if possible. I was not conscious of it but it must have been more apparent to others, as my half-sister later told me that she had always thought that I would become a priest. I had undoubtedly been enormously impressed by the devotion of the Maltese people where it was commonplace for ordinary lay people to attend Mass daily – in the case of fishermen Masses were attended as early as 4am before they went out fishing. I had also been greatly influenced by my contact with Archbishop Caruana and his Secretary, Michael Gonzi; and although I had not been conscious of it in Malta, I realise, looking back, that my vocation must have been initiated subconsciously at that time. However the Devil does his best to spoil vocations and, although I had never previously had any love affairs, it was at this time that I fell in love with a girl called 'Truffles' Parsons.

Warwick and my mother were still living in Park Lane; and Claire and her husband lived nearby. Since returning from Malta, I had taken a delightful little bachelor flat in Queen Street, Mayfair, and saw quite a lot of Roy and Claire. I often used to go with them in a large party with Jim Keenan and the Repton brothers to *Thé dansants* at the Grafton Galleries. We also saw a lot of Claire's great friend, Evelyn Laye, whose personal secretary she later became after the break-up of her first marriage. As we shall see later, when Jim followed me into the monastery at Downside, I was to have my leg pulled unmercifully about my friendship with the famous actress.

It was at the Grafton Galleries that I met 'Truffles' and her sister, Frieda. Perversely, although I thought I was in love with 'Truffles', I decided that I preferred Frieda, and then I realised that I did not really love either of them and that marriage was not for me. The story ends on a very sad note, as 'Truffles'

My sister and her husband Roy, two aunts and myself, c 1925

committed suicide soon afterwards – but not, I hasten to say, on my account.

My association with Archbishop Caruana, who was a Benedictine, naturally pointed me at that Order. Furthermore many of my brother officers had been to Downside, so I decided to go there and meet the Abbot.

I had visited Belmont Abbey, near Hereford, when I had been at a house party in the district and I had been very impressed with it. At Downside the Abbey church was incomplete: the nave had not been started, the tower only half built, and such features as the great East window not yet put in. Thus it was that at first sight I was more impressed with the buildings at Belmont. However, buildings are not everything, and I was immensely impressed by Abbot Ramsay.

Although a little aloof, he was one of the great Abbots of Downside. After obtaining a degree at Oxford, he was ordained Priest in the Church of England and became a Fellow of St Augustine's College, Canterbury, and later Vice-principal of the Theological College at Wells. Then in 1896 he was received

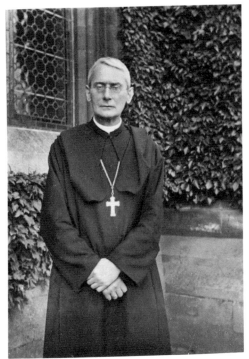

Dom Leander Ramsay

into the Catholic Church at Downside and entered the monastery the following year. In 1900 he was ordained a Catholic Priest and two years later was appointed Headmaster of the School, a post he held for 16 years. Finally, he had been elected third Abbot of Downside in 1922.

He was able to tell me something of the history of the English Benedictines. Whereas Belmont had been founded as a common Noviciate for all the houses of the English Congregation and had only recently become an independent abbey, Downside was one of the oldest Benedictine houses in England and a spiritual descendent of the pre-Reformation monasteries.

Furthermore, quite apart from the school, it was a centre of learning and had a comprehensive monastic library, though it is only recently that the books have all been housed together in a splendid new building.

Abbot Ramsay very wisely advised me to wait the few months until I had completed 10 years service in the Army, when I would qualify for a substantial gratuity. This money would come to the Community if I persevered; but more importantly it would be kept and returned to me if I did not succeed in my vocation to the monastic life, when I should find it very welcome.

So I soldiered on, and it was at this time that there occurred the ghastly incident of the sword scabbard. I was detailed for King's Guard and we were mounting in greatcoat order. In this order the sword scabbard, attached to the belt with slings, is worn under the greatcoat and the sword itself is sheathed in the scabbard through a slit in the greatcoat so that the hilt is outside. To avoid getting blanco all over myself under my greatcoat, Edgar Baird had given me the tip to just hook the scabbard onto the belt by its hook; but he omitted to mention that his servant nipped in the hook to ensure that it held. The Guard formed up on the barrack square and was inspected by the Adjutant, Sidney FitzGerald, accompanied by the Regimental Sergeant Major. I cannot recall who were the Captain and the other Subaltern but Joe Vandeleur was the Ensign. Sidney handed over the Guard to the Captain who then gave the order 'Fall In the Officers'. On this command the two Subalterns and the Ensign had to come to attention and step off smartly, drawing their swords at the same time and taking post in front of their respective Detachments. As I stepped off and drew my sword, my scabbard came off the hook and fell to the ground with a ghastly clatter. Of course nobody took any notice until the movement had been completed; but then Regimental Sergeant Major Harradine came forward from the supernumerary rank behind the Guard, picked up the offending scabbard with extreme distaste and handed it to the Sergeant-in-waiting to be carried off parade. It was subsequently wrapped in brown paper and sent round to the Officers' Guardroom at St James's where I was reunited with it.

Sidney FitzGerald as Adjutant

Naturally I was very apprehensive as to what Black Fitz would have to say, and quite by chance he dined with us on Guard that evening as the Captain's guest. In the event he was simply charming to us all and we enjoyed a very pleasant evening. When he had left, my brother officers all congratulated me on getting away with it. But no sooner had we dismounted Guard the following morning, than an Orderly came up to me and saluted: 'The Adjutant's compliments, Sir, and will you please report to him in the Orderly Room immediately.' When I reported to him, Sidney gave me a most frightful dressing down and, as a punishment, I was placed on indefinite Picquet Duty with the addition that I should attend every duty and fatigue which took place outside working hours. I cannot recall how long it went on, but it was sufficiently long for me to have to give up my little flat in Mayfair as I now had to live permanently in barracks.

By now it was generally known that I intended to leave the Army and become a priest and, although my brother officers respected this decision, I naturally came in for a certain amount of ribbing. In particular, I remember how Derek Murphy and Flash Kellett used to try and shock the future priest by using the most foul language imaginable. Needless to say, I did not rise to the bait.

In the spring of 1925 I was appointed Acting Regimental Adjutant for a few weeks while Bruce Reford was away for some reason. The Regimental Adjutant assists the Lieutenant Colonel at Regimental Headquarters and one of his duties is to receive newly-commissioned Officers and inspect all their uniforms to ensure that they fit properly and are correct in every detail. During the short time that I held this post, I received Second Lieutenant Andrew Montagu-Douglas-Scott, who was later to command the 1st Battalion in North Africa and at Anzio when I was to be Chaplain. Little did I know when I received him into the Regiment that we were to become such great friends.

The time for leaving the Army was now fast approaching; and the Regiment were very kind to me in that they undertook to take me back within one year of my leaving should I not succeed in my vocation. I was placed on the Reserve of Officers while I was a novice and it was only when I took my Simple Vows that I resigned from the Reserve.

Not long before this, Lord Plumer was appointed High Commissioner for Palestine. It was then a British Mandated Territory, so the job was really equivalent to a Military Governorship. Plum sent for me and did me the great honour of asking me to come out as his ADC again. He said: 'I know it is not good for his career for an officer to be away from his Regiment too long, but I promise to square it with the Regimental Lieutenant Colonel and you will suffer no loss of seniority or preferment.' I had to tell him that I had decided to leave the Army and become a priest. He replied: 'Well, I was prepared to argue with you, but you are leaving the Army for the only thing worthwhile. If God spares me, I will be at your Ordination.' Sadly, he died before I was ordained and instead I attended his funeral at Westminster Abbey dressed in black clerical frockcoat and silk top hat.

My resignation took effect from 12th August 1925, but I had a few weeks leave due to me and was therefore able to say good-bye to my family and brother officers and present myself at Downside as a postulant nearly a month before that. It was a farewell to arms – my Army career was over, as I thought, and an entirely new chapter in my life lay before me.

Chapter 6

Noviciate

On the 15th July 1925, I arrived at Downside as a postulant. A postulant is one who seeks admission – one who is knocking at the door. St Benedict says in his Rule: 'To him that cometh to change his life, let not an easy entrance be granted. If he that cometh persevere in knocking, and after four or five days seem patiently to endure the difficulty made about his coming in, and to persist in his petition, let entrance be granted him, and let him be in the guest house for a few days.' I am glad to say that the Rule is no longer enforced literally; but postulants still lodge in the monastery for varying times while they follow the monastic life, before being 'clothed' in the 'habit' and entering the noviciate.

I learnt afterwards that my arrival had in fact caused quite a stir and unknown to me my fellow novices observed with interest from a high window the arrival of the young Guards Officer!

I was received by Abbot Ford, the first Abbot of Downside and long since retired. Before his time the Superiors had only been Priors. Abbot Ford conducted me to my cell, a room on the third floor of the monastery next to the Novices' common room. Those who have visited the ruins of medieval monasteries know that the monks slept together in a dormitory or 'dorter'. The Rule says: 'Let the monks sleep each one in a separate bed, receiving bedding suitable to their manner of life, as the Abbot shall appoint. If possible, let all sleep in one place; but if the number do not permit of this, let them repose by tens or twenties with the seniors who have charge of them. Let a candle burn constantly in the cell until morning. Let them sleep clothed, and girded with belts or cords – but not with knives at their sides, lest perchance they wound themselves in their sleep – and thus be always ready, so that when the signal is given they may rise without delay, and hasten each to forestall the other in going to the Work of God, yet with all gravity and modesty. Let not the younger brethren have their beds by themselves, but among the seniors. And when they rise for the Work of God, let them gently encourage one another because of the excuses of the drowsy.' As late as 1341 the General Chapter of the English Benedictines was repeating the prohibition on separate cells; but in modern times the Rule has been relaxed in this respect.

I was somewhat downcast by the sparse furnishing of my room but, as an old soldier, I was used to making myself as comfortable as possible. It therefore came naturally to me to tip the monastery servants lavishly to provide me with additional furniture including a comfortable armchair. I cunningly did this before handing in all my money to the Bursar. Of course this shows how little idea I had of humility and the monastic way of life. Monks may own great possessions in common but nothing individually. To quote the Rule: 'The vice of private ownership is above all to be cut off from the roots. Let none presume to give or receive anything as their own, either book or writing-tablet or pen, or anything whatsoever; since they are permitted to have neither body nor will in their own power. But all that it is necessary they may hope to receive from the father of the monastery: nor are they allowed to keep anything which the Abbot has not given, or at least permitted them to have. Let all things be common to all. But if any one shall be found to indulge in this most baneful vice, and after one or two admonitions do not amend, let him be subjected to correction.' The Rule continues: 'As it is written: "Distribution was made to every man, according as he had need". Herein we do not say that there should be respecting of persons – God forbid – but consideration for infirmities. Let him therefore, that hath need of less give thanks to God, and not be grieved: and let him who requireth more be humbled for his infirmity, and not made proud by the kindness shown to him: and so all the members of the family shall be at peace. Above all, let not the evil of murmuring shew itself by the slightest word or sign on any account whatsoever. If anyone be found guilty herein, let him be subjected to severe punishment.' The Bursar held the money of postulants and novices in trust and returned it to them if they gave up and left the monastery. However, on solemn profession all a monk's money is given to the monastery absolutely and his will is made in favour of the monastery. This is varied to some extent in cases where a monk enters later in life and has dependents to be provided for.

The time of postulancy differed according to circumstances, very young lads being required to wait longer than more mature ones. Rather like recruits joining at the Guards Depot, it was also necessary to form a squad or class of novices to start together. I was then 27 years of age and had been through three years of war, so I was fairly mature and only remained a postulant for two months.

On 20th September 1925, I was 'clothed' by Abbot Ramsay. This is a solemn ceremony in which lay clothes are discarded and the postulant is clothed by the Abbot in the monastic habit. The ceremony symbolises conversion of life.

We postulants wore the tunic and scapular but no hood and had our places in the front of the choirstalls. But on the day of our clothing, we were dressed only in clerical suits. After Vespers the Abbot was vested in cope and mitre and we were led out of the choir by the Novicemaster to kneel in front of the Abbot who questioned us in Latin as follows: 'What is your request, dearly beloved brothers?' We replied in turn: 'If it be God's will and yours, I desire to save my soul amongst you under the rule of the Most Holy Father Benedict.' The Abbot then explained to us how many and great were the difficulties of religious life and concluded by asking: 'What think you? Do you still stand by your resolution?' We each replied: 'Such is my will and desire relying on the help of Divine Grace'. To which the whole Community replied: 'Amen'. The Abbot then knelt at the foot of the altar to intone the *Veni, Creator Spiritus*, the ancient hymn calling upon the Holy Ghost which is used on all the most solemn occasions, such as Ordinations, Weddings and Papal

My Noviciate: Wulstan Phillipson, Clement Hayes, myself, Leander Donovan, Andrew Snelgrove, Ralph Russell and Jerome O'Connell with our Novicemaster, Dom Richard Davy

Elections, etc. After the first verse, the Abbot rose and sat at his faldstool and, while the Choir continued with the hymn, each postulant knelt in front of him in turn and his coat was removed and he was clothed by the Abbot in tunic, scapular, cowl and hood. After this the Abbot recited a number of prayers concluding with: 'O God, who didst command Thy chosen servant the Blessed Benedict to withdraw himself from the world and fight for Thee alone; grant, we beseech Thee, to these Thy servants hastening into Thy service under his Rule, that final victory which is only won by a steadfast perseverance. Through Christ Our Lord. Amen.' The Abbot then gave each of us the Kiss of Peace and we knelt before him to receive our religious names and his blessing. Finally, we each kissed the Abbot's ring in token of our obedience and were taken back to our places in choir by the Novicemaster.

Although the tonsure is no longer given as such, we had to have a simple close-cropping of the head rather like a Guards recruit. There are remarkable similarities with the Army as the senior monks are permitted to wear their hair substantially longer than the novices, just as there is a big difference between recruits and trained soldiers in this respect.

My noviciate consisted of seven including myself and they were certainly an interesting and assorted bunch.

First there was Leander Donovan, an ordained priest aged 31, who had been a priest for five years in the Middlesbrough diocese and had at this late stage decided to try his vocation as a monk. He was an Irishman from Cork who had been at University in both Cork and Dublin and to the Seminary at Leeds. Leander was very much on his dignity with us because of his priesthood which was interesting as St Benedict is very tough about priests entering the monastery: 'If any one in priestly order ask to be received into the monastery, let not consent be too quickly granted him; but if he persist in his request, let him know that he will have to observe all the discipline of the Rule, and that nothing will be relaxed in his favour. Let him nevertheless be allowed to stand next to the Abbot, to give the blessing, and to say Mass, if the Abbot bid him do so. Otherwise, let him presume to do nothing, knowing that he is subject to the discipline of the Rule; but rather let him give an example of humility to all. And if there be a question of any appointment, or other business in the monastery, let him expect the position due to him according to the time of his entrance, and not that which was yielded to him out of reverence for the priesthood.' In St Benedict's time, hardly any of the monks were priests whereas in modern times nearly all the monks are ordained after their solemn profession, so the bit about standing next to the Abbot did not apply to Leander; but the basic principle that his seniority dated from his entrance into the monastery still held.

He was solemnly professed in 1929 and became Novicemaster from 1933 to 1939. He also taught Moral Theology. For the remaining 35 years of his life, he looked after two local parishes from the monastery. For many years he was also one of the school confessors.

Next there was Clement Hayes, a Lancastrian aged only 18, who had been educated by the Christian Brothers at Clifton. He was so young that he had been kept as a postulant for a whole year. He was rather an ebullient character with a typical North Country humour – more of him anon. After ordination he taught in the school for a short time and also did parish work. In 1937 he was sent to our daughter house at Ealing, from whence he entered the Army as a chaplain in 1939 serving in North Africa, Italy and later in India. He returned to Ealing after the War; and when Ealing became an independent Abbey in 1947, he transferred his stability.

I should perhaps explain that monasteries increase and multiply on the cell system. A mother house founds a daughter house to which are sent monks under obedience. Monks take a vow of stability to a particular house and must stay in that house all their lives. This is made very clear in Chapter I of the Rule: 'It is well known that there are four kinds of monks. The first are the Cenobites: that is those in monasteries, who live under a rule or abbot. The second are the Anchorites or Hermits: that is those who, not in the first fervour of religious life, but after long probation in the monastery, have learned by the help and experience of many to fight against the devil; and going forth well armed from the ranks of their brethren to the single-handed combat of the desert, are able, without the support of others, to fight by the strength of their own arm, God helping them, against the vices of the flesh and their evil thoughts. A third and most baneful kind of monks are the Sarabites, who have been tried by no rule nor by the experience of a master, as gold in the furnace; but being soft as lead, and still serving the world in their works, are known by their tonsure to lie to God. These in twos and threes, or even singly, without a shepherd, shut up, not in the Lord's sheepfolds, but in their own, make a law to themselves in the pleasure of their own desires; whatever they think fit or choose to do, that they call holy; and what they like not, that they consider unlawful. The fourth kind of monks are those called Girovagi, who spend all their live-long wandering about divers provinces, staying in different cells for three or four days at a time, ever roaming, with no stability, given up to their own pleasures and to the snares of gluttony, and worse in all things than the Sarabites. Of the most wretched life of these it is better to say nothing than to speak. Leaving them alone therefore, let us set to work, by the help of God, to lay down a rule for the Cenobites, that is the strongest kind of monks.'

It is therefore under obedience that monks may be sent by their Abbot to a daughter house or indeed on a job such as to be chaplain to a convent. When the daughter house is considered to be sufficiently well-established and provided there are enough volunteers who are willing to transfer their vow of stability to the new house, it is granted its independence and the Abbot presides over its first Chapter at which a new independent Superior is elected and he then transfers the property and a reasonable proportion of the mother house's funds to the new independent foundation. At this point, monks who have been sent to the new house under obedience have the right to return to the mother house and those who wish to join the new house from the mother house may ask to do so. While the new house is dependent upon the mother Abbey, it is called a Priory with a Conventual Prior appointed by the Abbot. After independence it continues as a Priory with an independent Prior elected by the new Community; but when Rome considers that it is sufficiently well-established as an independent house it is granted abbatial status and the superior becomes an Abbot with the right to mitre and crozier.

I come now to Ralph Russell, known to generations of Downside boys affectionately as 'Tusky' owing to the prominence of his front teeth. 'Tusky', who came from Devon, was then 22 years of age and just down from Oxford where he had taken 1st Class Honours in Classical 'Mods'. He was an OG (Old Gregorian), meaning that he had been a boy in the school, and he had won the Gregorian Medal in 1921. He spent his whole life at Downside, apart from a short spell at Worth before the War, mostly teaching English and Religious Instruction in the school and also as Professor of Dogmatic Theology in the monastery for nearly 20 years. He was also Novicemaster from 1956 to 1962.

Generations of boys remember his RI (Religious Instruction) classes for his 'Man in the train'. In teaching the truths of the

Catholic Faith, he was insistent that the boys should be apostolic and able to answer simple questions from strangers. He postulated that one was travelling in a train when a fellow traveller suddenly addressed one thus: 'I perceive, Sir, that you are a Roman Catholic. Can you please explain to me the Virgin Birth?' or some other dogma. It was never quite clear how the stranger perceived that one was an RC but that did not really matter. He was a man of great holiness and came to be loved and revered by monks and boys alike and indeed by a wide circle of friends outside the monastery.

Next we have Andrew Snelgrove, a Canadian from Coburg, Ontario, aged 24 and a recent convert to Catholicism. He had been to Toronto University and was received into the Church while there. After gaining his BA in 1924, he went as a postulant to Portsmouth Priory, Rhode Island, USA, but subsequently came to Downside still as a postulant for Portsmouth, though in the event he was 'clothed' with me for Downside in September 1925. After his noviciate, he was sent for four years to study at the College of Sant' Anselmo in Rome. On his return he taught at Downside, Worth and Ealing before becoming an Army Chaplain on the outbreak of War. He served in Algeria in 1942; and later was posted to Pirbright Camp which has since become the Guards Depot. After the War he returned to Ealing and then to Worth where he died at the early age of 47 in 1948.

I now come to Wulstan Phillipson who became and remained a great friend. 'Woolly' as we called him in the Noviciate because of his close-cropped black hair, was only 18 and came from Dublin's fair city. He had been educated at Mount St Benedict's, Gorey, a school founded by Downside in Co Wicklow in 1907 but which had to be disbanded during the 'Troubles' because some of the staff became politically involved. He went on to Trinity College, Dublin, and then tried his hand for a short time as an actor at the famous Abbey Theatre. Wulstan had only had one year at Trinity and so, in accordance with the custom with young monks who joined the monastery before going to university, he was sent to Christ's College, Cambridge, in 1928 after completing his three years in the Noviciate. He obtained his BA in 1931. Downside kept a House of Residence at Cambridge, called Benet House, presided over by a senior monk, where young monks stayed while attending the university. In those days they had a very strict regime and did not have much time with their fellow lay undergraduates outside lecture times. It was of course also a centre and link for lay OGs who were up at the university and the senior monk acted to some extent as an extra university chaplain.

Throughout his life Wulstan maintained his deep love of the theatre and was responsible for numerous plays in the school during the 45 years which he spent teaching English and Religious Instruction at Downside, only broken by a short spell at Worth before the War. He actually came to Downside with the hope of returning to Gorey which he had loved so much as a boy; but although the property has been retained by Downside, the school was not re-opened and he was never sent there.

'Wappy', as he was nicknamed by the boys and which superseded his earlier nickname in the monastery, was a born public relations man and an old-fashioned Irish match-maker. He had a deep and simple faith which he successfully conveyed to large numbers of boys who kept up with him after they had left the school. Naturally they wanted him to officiate at their weddings and later at the christening of their children and he had the ability to get on with most of the wives. He loved society and it must be admitted that he had a weakness for the table, but he did an immense amount of good in keeping in touch with old boys and in persuading wives (often non-Catholic) that Downside was a first class school and that they need have no fear in entrusting their little darlings to the monks. As the years went by the little book in which he recorded all his weddings and christenings grew and he was always trying to introduce his favourite OGs to the sisters or daughters of other OGs. He had no hesitation in writing to famous actors and playrights to obtain permission to perform a play or on behalf of any boy aspiring to a stage career; and to name but two, he became close friends with Christopher Fry and Sir Alec Guinness. His pleasure was enormous when one of his old boys, Barry England, wrote a play 'Conduct Unbecoming' which became a Box Office success overnight in the West End.

Last but not least we come to Jerome O'Connell, who arrived in his Rolls Royce which he donated to the monastery! I have used the professed religious names rather than Christian names throughout; but Jerome was in fact Sir John O'Connell, an Irish solicitor and JP who had been knighted in 1914 and was then aged 57. He had been educated by the Jesuits at Belvedere College and went on to Trinity College, Dublin. He was on the Senate of Dublin University and on the Boards of numerous charitable bodies. His wife, to whom he had been married for 24 years, had died early in 1925, and they had made a compact that whichever one survived the other should enter the religious life – hence his arrival as a postulant at Downside.

He was a very small man indeed and the butt of many jokes on the part of his fellow novices. He was so short that when he stood behind the altar it looked as though he were kneeling. He did not succeed in the monastic vocation and left Downside before Christmas that year. He turned however to the secular clergy and was eventually ordained priest by Cardinal Bourne at Westminster in 1929.

Such then were my fellow novices who were clothed with me on 20th September 1925. There were of course other novices from the previous years who overlapped with us to some extent, such as Matthew Kehoe and Hubert van Zeller of whom I will speak later.

I had asked Abbot Ramsay if I might use my real name on joining the monastery and starting a new life. However when I told him what it was, he at once said it was much too difficult and decided that I should continue to call myself Brookes. On entering religion one is given a religious name and I had hoped to take one of my own names, John Charles Hugo. However, it was decreed by the Abbot that I should take the name Rudesind; and I am very glad as it is one which is not common among the English Benedictines. During my time there has never been another Rudesind in any of the other Houses with whom I might be confused!

It will be apparent that with the exception of Leander and myself and of course Sir John O'Connell, the novices were all extremely young. Matthew Kehoe and Hubert van Zeller who were a year ahead of us were 19 and 20 respectively and even Adrian Morey, who had been clothed in 1923, was only 21. In those days young men were very much less sophisticated than they are now and tended to retain a rather schoolboyish sense of humour. I was talking recently to Adrian Morey, who is now Master of Benet House at Cambridge, and he reminded me how he and Gregory Murray were often sent out of the refectory for giggling! We older novices and particularly poor Sir John were therefore to some extent the butt of their jokes, though there was nothing malicious about it. A typical example was when I was having a bath and Matthew and some of the others climbed up and threw cold water over me through the fanlight. In those days we all wore shorts under our habits and one of the novices decided that another's were too long, so he cut off the ends and put the pieces in the victim's breviary so that they fell out when he opened it in choir next day. Matthew was always baiting poor Leander, who was so much on his dignity as a priest, by such puerile pranks as putting pepper in his tea!

Three years are spent in the Noviciate, the first year being termed the 'canonical year'. A year and a day after 'clothing' one makes one's simple profession for three years. After two years as a professed novice, one leaves the Noviciate and enters the Juniorate where one remains until Ordination. After three years in Simple Vows, a monk goes forward to make his Solemn Profession which is for life. It sounds very solemn and irrevocable, which indeed it is, but there is ample time to test one's vocation and for the Community to consider whether one is suited. An unsuitable person can be like a maggot in an apple, so the Community take great care to ensure that a person has a true vocation to the life before accepting him for solemn profession.

Postulants are accepted at the discretion of the Abbot; but novices may not be 'clothed' without the consent of the Council of Seniors. Half this Council is elected by the Chapter and the other half may be nominated by the Abbot.

About a month before the novices are due to take their Simple Vows, every member of the resident Community must privately see the Abbot and give his views and then again each must, one by one, visit the Council. After this the Abbot consults his Council and they consider the report of the Novicemaster on each novice. Needless to say, great weight is given to the latter. Finally a secret vote is taken by the whole Chapter, which comprises all the solemnly professed monks. The ballot is taken with black and white beans; and I imagine that the balloting in London clubs with black and white balls owes its origin to this ancient monastic custom. However, unlike the club rule that 'one black ball excludes', only a two thirds clear majority is required; nor may the scrutineers divulge the number of votes cast. Each novice is simply voted 'In' or 'Out'. A similar procedure of consultation and voting is carried out prior to Solemn Profession, except that in this case it is the Junior Master's reports which are considered.

Dom Richard Davy was our Novicemaster and was entirely responsible for us. In those days, the novices were very strictly segregated especially during the first year. There was virtually no contact with the Community except on great Feasts, nor indeed with the boys in the school. Dom Richard was a kindly man if not very inspiring and he did his best to be strict with us.

The daily routine in the monastery was rather harder than it is now and we rose at 5am for Matins, Lauds and Prime. Novices took turns at being Duty Caller which meant getting up, washing and dressing before 5am and then ringing the bell before going round the entire monastery, knocking on every door and calling out *Benedicamus Domino* to which the sleeper replied *Deo Gratias*. There was an amusing incident a year or so later when Simon van Zeller followed his brother Hubert into the monastery and was a novice. He happened to be Duty Caller at the time when the clocks were changed at the end of Summertime. Unfortunately he forgot to put his own clock back and proceeded to ring the bell and go round rousing the entire community at 4am instead of 5am much to everyone's consternation.

Matins, Lauds and Prime lasted until 6.40am when we had half an hour mental prayer followed by the Noviciate Mass said by Dom Richard in St Isidore's chapel. We received Holy Communion at this Mass as in those days everyone had to fast from midnight before receiving. Breakfast was at 8am and we then worked in the Sacristy until 9am when there was Terce followed by the Conventual High Mass. After that there was more work in the Sacristy, putting away vestments, and so on, followed by Latin studies under Dom Ambrose Agius.

At 11am we had a compulsory glass of milk and went on the *Corpus* walk for about 20 minutes round the grounds. This was led by the Senior novice and we were allowed to talk. It was the first time we had been able to talk since rising at 5am. There followed half an hour private reading in our rooms and then at 12 noon there was a Conference in the Noviciate Room given by the Novicemaster on the Rule of St Benedict, the Constitutions of the English Congregation and other liturgical matters. After this came a visit to the Blessed Sacrament before None which was followed immediately by lunch at 1pm.

Lunch in the refectory was in silence during which we were read to by a Reader. Another monk is Server and during their week of office these two eat separately after the Community have finished their meal. The Server is responsible for seeing that all the monks are served and is assisted by a number of other monks who pass round the plates. After the second course when he has ascertained that everyone has finished eating, he comes into the centre and bows to the Abbot at the High Table, whereupon the latter strikes a bell for all to stand and sing grace.

After luncheon the Community adjourn to the Calefactory for coffee where they may talk. Nowadays the novices do likewise but, when I was a novice, we were only allowed to take coffee on Sundays and great Feasts and even then the senior novice had to ask first the Novicemaster and then the Abbot if the novices might take coffee. We were allowed to speak to the Community if we came to coffee but, like newly-joined ensigns in an Officers' Mess, it was very much a case of only speaking when one was spoken to!

At 2.15pm we changed into rough clothes for Manual Labour for an hour and a half until 3.45pm. This was normally work in the garden directed by the monk in charge according to our capabilities – I am afraid I was not very capable and must have been a problem to him. In bad weather the work was indoors, cleaning and polishing; and I remember particularly being detailed to clean out the 'loos' for which I changed into PT gear. I think this chore was specially selected for me to bring the Guards Officer down a peg or two, as I do not recall any of the others being called upon to do it.

We sometimes undertook quite major projects such as digging a trench in which to bury cables from the power house to the school – in those days we generated our own electricity. One day when we were working in the garden, Matthew and Wulstan – both hot-headed Irishmen – had a difference of opinion. One had a spade and the other a pick axe and they went at each other and had to be separated by 'Tusky' who almost got his teeth knocked out in the fracas!

Another time we were levelling the top cricket ground and the OTC were drilling nearby. There was at that time a boy in the school called Gubbins which was a bit of a joke among the novices. We happened to hear Cadet Gubbins being berated by a Sergeant which caused extreme merriment among us, for which we were sent down by the Novicemaster and later had to recite the seven penitential psalms. On another occasion we were disciplined for laughing at Sir John O'Connell when he was carpet-beating, instead of getting on with our own work. What the Novicemaster did not know was that Sir John was giving us a demonstration of how the orphans were beaten in some Dublin institution with which he had been connected!

After Manual Labour we had a bath or in summertime went for a swim in the open-air Petre swimming pool, and I recall that we taught Andrew Snelgrove to swim.

Sometimes we played hockey or tennis instead of Manual Labour or even played the 'Ball Game' which had been imported from Douai and was a sort of 'fives' played with a hard ball and wooden bat. The wall in the Ball Place is an exact copy of that at Douai and was presumably erected to retain the memory of Douai as well as to enable the game to be played. Abbot Hicks was an expert and played with the Prince of Wales when he visited Downside on a tour of the Duchy of Cornwall.

On Sundays and occasionally on a weekday there was a Noviciate Walk led by the Novicemaster or a *Gravis monachus* (a senior monk). We went out of the grounds but Dom Richard seldom went further than Emborough and of course we wore our black clerical suits. On these walks it was understood among the novices that the two walking with Dom Richard should be replaced after a decent interval by two others; and if the replacements were too engrossed in their own conversation to notice the passage of time, despairing signals would be sent out by the pair trapped with Dom Richard whose conversation tended to revolve round Cardinals and the Papal Curia.

Tea was in the refectory not in the calefactory as it is now, and the novices ate in silence though the seniors were allowed to talk. After tea there was spiritual reading from a book selected by the Novicemaster – usually *The Lives of the Saints*, especially *The Little Flower* (Saint Teresa of Lisieux) or *The Curé d'Ars*. The book was passed round and we took turns at reading, while Dom Richard made pertinent comments. We then did more work in the Sacristy, followed by half an hour's mental prayer before Vespers at 6.30pm. One of the jobs in the Sacristy was to tend the candles of the High Altar which had false centres which had to be replaced when they were used up. Adrian was inclined to gamble on whether there was enough left to last another Matins or Vespers; and I recall one dreadful occasion when, just as the whole community turned towards the altar to sing the *Magnificat* at Vespers, the candles popped out – not just one but all six one after another, to the chagrin of the Novicemaster who was responsible for seeing that his novices kept the liturgical accessories in order.

If you were guilty of some minor fault in choir, the Abbot would tap you on the shoulder and you would have to leave your place and kneel in the middle of the choir facing the altar to do penance until the Abbot gave the sign for you to return to your place. On one occasion at Matins, Abbot Ramsay had evidently got out of bed on the wrong side that morning and decided that the novices on his side of the choir were not singing loudly enough, so he sent them out one by one to do penance in the middle, the last one being Leander, who was very indignant, saying later: 'I don't think the Abbot realises that I am a priest.'

Supper followed Vespers at 7pm and at 7.30pm there was *Corona* when we sat round the Novicemaster in a semi-circle in the Noviciate room and had recreational conversation led by Dom Richard, which was extremely boring. Sometimes in the summer this took the form of a stroll round the garden.

At 8.30pm there was Compline, at the end of which we solemnly proceeded from the choir to the Lady Chapel where we sang the *Salve Regina* or other seasonal anthem to Our Lady. This was the last service of the day and was followed by the *Summum Silentium* (the Great Silence) and bed, as we had to be up again at 5am! So strictly was the Great Silence kept in those days that we all wore special felt slippers instead of shoes from after Compline until breakfast the next day.

One final duty of the novices was to lock up the Abbey church after Compline. I have mentioned Clement Hayes as being extremely young and rather irresponsible; and when he was on this duty, I felt it prudent to check up that he had done the job properly. However he discovered that I was doing this; and got his own back by waiting until I had locked up when it was my turn for this duty, and then unlocking the doors and pulling my leg by telling me that I had not locked the doors properly!

Sometime in 1926 during my first year as a novice, dear old Jim Keenan arrived as a postulant. Jim had left the Regiment at the end of 1924 and gone out to the Argentine as an Exchange broker. He found the life very boring and came back to England after 18 months and decided to try his vocation at Downside, where he took the name of Brother Caedmon.

Jim had a keen Irish sense of humour and, needless to say, I was the butt of much of his good-natured wit. In particular he regaled the novices with stories of my supposed romance with Miss Evelyn Laye, the well known actress. On one occasion there was an article by Miss Laye in one of the glossy magazines, which had an illustration showing her in leotards doing fitness exercises, whereupon Brother Caedmon announced to the assembled novices: 'Brother Rudesind taught her those!'

One evening I went into the boxroom in the noviciate after Compline to fetch something and I was locked in by Brother Caedmon. As it was in the Great Silence, to bang on the door would have been unthinkable – better to remain locked up all night. All I could do was to scratch quietly on the door and wait until someone eventually heard and released me.

Sadly Jim did not persevere. He went on holiday to Lourdes before being 'clothed' and decided not to proceed. I rather lost touch with him after that but he tried his vocation as a monk once more after the Second War, this time at Ealing, where he was clothed as a novice. However, before he was due to make his Simple Profession, the Council decided that he was too old to continue and he had to leave the monastery.

Once a week there was a Chapter of Faults, held in the Crypt chapel under the Novicemaster, at which we accused ourselves of infringements of the Rule and were given penances – sometimes Dom Richard would remind us of offences we had forgotten. At one time the whole Community took part in the Chapter of Faults; but it is no longer practised, not even by the novices.

Rather like recruits at the Guards Depot, whose pleasures tend to be restricted to such simple matters as food in the NAAFI, our highlights consisted of the occasional relaxation of the strict regime under which we lived. In wintertime on great Feasts, Dom Richard would take us to a nearby farm for a special teaparty. We would sit round a roaring fire eating hot buttered scones. In summertime, the great treat was the outing to Bonham at Stourhead in Wiltshire, where we had permission to picnic in the grounds and bathe in the lake. There was always a magnificent ham on the table and if Dom Richard were not with us, we were given cigars or cigarettes to smoke. I need hardly say that smoking was never allowed – not even at Christmas.

The Christmas holidays were a great time when the Community moved down into the boys' refectory, where there was an enormous log fire in the baronial fireplace, and the novices were allowed to talk to each other and to the community. I should mention that we were not allowed in each other's rooms; and, if we had to speak to another novice in his room, we had to leave one leg outside the door! No long conversations were permitted and no particular friendships.

The first year novices had no holiday at all but the professed novices went on a Noviciate holiday which was usually at Ashington Farm, near Lynton, on Exmoor. Dom Vincent Corney was in charge and we spent most of our time walking and swimming. Sometimes we had bicycles and one year we even cycled the whole way there and back.

We were always invited to tea on a Sunday by the MacDermots at a nearby farm. One time I was walking there in my black clericals and thumbed a lift from a smart chauffeur-driven limousine in which there turned out to be the Dean of Winchester and his lady. We entered upon an animated conversation when to my horror the car slowed again and there was Andrew also thumbing a lift. They agreed to take him; but the conversation flagged somewhat after this!

Such then were my days in the Noviciate. I duly took my Simple Vows before Abbot Ramsay on 21st September 1926, a year and a day after my 'clothing'; and I thus became a Professed Novice or Junior in the Noviciate, where I remained for two more years while studying Philosophy under Dom Oliver Brayden. On the day upon which I took my Simple Vows, I resigned from the Regular Army Reserve of Officers.

Chapter 7

Monk and Schoolmaster

As a Professed Novice, I remained under the Novicemaster but the discipline was very slightly relaxed. For example, I did not go on the *Corpus* walk and, as mentioned earlier, I was able to go on the Noviciate holiday.

After two years, I finally left the Noviciate and became a Junior in the Community. I now came under the Junior Master, who for my first year as a Junior was Dom Hugh Connolly, a gentle, kindly monk; and I embarked on my four years Theology study. Dom Edmund Kendal taught me Moral Theology and Dom David Knowles Dogmatic Theology. In the Noviciate we had received a Conference daily from the Novicemaster, now in the Community we attended the Abbot's weekly Conference and in addition the Juniors attended a weekly Conference given by the Junior Master.

In March 1929, Abbot Ramsay died; and on 11th April Dom John Chapman was elected fourth Abbot of Downside. Not yet being solemnly professed, I was not a member of the Chapter and therefore I was not present at his election.

Abbot Chapman was very different from his predecessor. He was mercurial, versatile, very learned and rather unpredictable. He was the son of an Anglican Archdeacon and was himself ordained an Anglican Deacon before being received into the Catholic Church at the London Oratory in 1890 at the age of 25. He spent a few months trying his vocation as a Jesuit and then received the Benedictine habit at Maredsous Abbey in Belgium. He served as a Chaplain in France during the Great War and in 1919 transferred his stability to Downside. He was a pianist and had the disconcerting habit of practising by running the fingers of his right hand up and down his left hand sleeve. His reign only lasted four years as, unknown to us, he was very ill and he died of leukemia in 1933.

On 21st September 1929, I made my Solemn Profession before Abbot Chapman; but before this I was allowed 12 days holiday at home, my first visit home or indeed outside monastic supervision since I had arrived as a Postulant four years earlier. On our return from holiday, those making their Solemn Profession were given a week's Retreat by Dom David.

The day before we were to make our Solemn Profession, we Juniors were led into the Chapter Room before the assembled Community by the Junior Master and we knelt before the Abbot who once again told us of the many great difficulties of the monastic life, concluding with these words: 'Dearly beloved brethren, you have now for four years observed the Rule under which you wish to live, and the Constitutions of our Congregation. You know, therefore, what are the difficulties and burdens of the monastic law. If you can keep this law, enter amongst us; if not, you are free to depart.' He then pointed to two chairs on one of which was laid a set of lay clothes and on the other a monastic cowl and asked us to choose. We each replied: 'These and many other similar matters I have pondered in my mind, and after much thought and deliberation I now seek my profession, for with the help of Divine Grace I desire to live and die in the habit of our Holy Father St Benedict.' The Abbot then declared that on the next day he would receive us to profession.

For the ceremony of Solemn Profession, a special Pontifical High Mass was sung. We Juniors were in our usual places wearing new tunics but our old scapulars and hoods. At the Offertory, we were led out by our Junior Master into the middle of the Choir while the Abbot faced us sitting on the faldstool in front of the High Altar. Each one of us in turn sung our profession in Latin: 'In the name of Our Lord Jesus Christ. Amen. In the year one thousand nine hundred and twenty nine after Our Blessed Lord's Nativity, and on the twenty-first day of the month of September, I, Brother Rudesind Brookes of Mayfair in the county of London, in the Diocese of Westminster in

England, promise before God and his Saints, Stability and Conversion of Manners, and Obedience according to the Rule of our Holy Father Saint Benedict and the Constitutions of the English Congregation approved by the Holy See under the Right Reverend Dom John Chapman, Abbot of the monastery of St Gregory, and his successors in this monastery of St Gregory of the said Order and Congregation in the Diocese of Clifton, in the presence of the Right Reverend Dom John Chapman, Abbot, and the monks of the aforesaid monastery. In witness whereof I have written this document or petition with my own hand on the day, month and year above-mentioned.'

When we had all sung our vows, the Abbot prayed: 'Let us pray, beloved brethren, that what these brothers have just promised in words, they may successfully accomplish in deeds, through the help of Our Lord Jesus Christ, who with the Father and Holy Spirit, liveth and reigneth, God, for ever and ever, Amen.' We then stood in a row facing the Abbot at the altar and, helped by the Cantors, sung the *Suscipe* three times, moving forward a little and singing in Latin on a higher note each time: 'Receive me, O Lord, according to Thy Word and I shall live, and in my expectation, never let me be confounded.'

Each of us in turn then ascended the steps of the altar and signed our Profession which we had previously written out on parchment in our own hands. These were counter-signed by the Abbot and witnessed by the Secretary to the Council. The parchments were then rolled up and tied with ribbon by the Master of Ceremonies and each of us placed our own Profession on the corporal, a special linen cloth on the altar during Mass on which are placed the Chalice and Sacred Host.

We then returned to the middle of the Choir and lay prostrate on a black pall at the four corners of which were placed four lighted requiem candles, signifying our death to the world, while the Choir sang the Litany of the Saints on our behalf, followed by the Lord's Prayer and a number of other prayers. We rose and knelt on the bottom step of the altar while the Abbot blessed our new Habits. The Abbot then knelt to intone the *Veni, Creator Spiritus.* Rising after the first verse and sitting on the faldstool, he removed our old habits and put on the new ones while the Choir continued with the hymn.

The Abbot gave each of us the Kiss of Peace; and the whole Community having come out of the Choir, we knelt in turn in front of each of them and received the Kiss of Peace. Finally the Abbot put up our hoods and pinned them, before giving us his Blessing. We were led back to our places by the Junior Master and the Mass continued as usual. For three days we had to keep our hoods pinned up and could not speak to anyone except the Abbot or our confessor and could not even sing in Choir or receive Communion. This symbolised our descent into the tomb. On the third day, at the Conventual High Mass *Agnus Dei,* the Abbot unpinned our hoods and we received Communion.

After my Solemn Profession I continued as a Junior, until my Ordination in 1931, but there was a change in the Junior Master and Dom David Knowles succeeded Dom Hugh.

Dom David, who was later to become Professor of Medieval History at Cambridge and then Regius Professor of Modern History and President of the Royal Historical Society, was a remarkable man. He was two years older than me, had been a boy in the school at Downside and had entered the monastery on leaving the school. After Solemn Profession, he had been sent to Christ's College, Cambridge, where he obtained First Class Honours in both parts of the Classical Tripos, with Distinction in Philosophy. He returned to Downside in 1922 to be ordained and was then sent for a year to the College of Sant' Anselmo in Rome. On his return from Rome he started to teach Classics in the school. He was a high-powered person who was also deeply spiritual and came to exercise a considerable influence over the Juniors.

During the 15 centuries since St Benedict wrote his Rule for monks, there has been an ever-recurring tendency for the strict interpretation of the Rule to be eased and, as a consequence, from time to time there have sprung up movements to return to the strict practice of the Rule. A good example is the Cistercian Order which was basically a return to following the Rule in its strictest sense. The Cistercians retire at 7pm, rising at 2am for the Night Office and then do not return to bed. Other reforms have included rising at midnight for the Night Office, then returning to bed and rising again at daybreak for Lauds and Prime – a very hard routine. Our English Benedictines rise at 5am and sing the Night Office followed immediately by Lauds and Prime. It may appear slack, but there are good practical reasons for this routine. The stricter reformed Benedictines and Cistercians do not normally run schools as we do, which entail many monks not retiring before 11.30pm or even midnight.

In our own country which was evangelised by St Augustine and his 40 monks, the monks being missionaries, naturally built their monasteries in the centres of population, so that in the Middle Ages there were great Abbeys at Canterbury, Westminster, Gloucester, Peterborough, etc. To someone who wished to keep the strict Rule this was highly unsuitable, so Cistercian monasteries were all founded in remote parts of the country like Tintern, Caldy Island and the Yorkshire dales. One example is Fountains Abbey which was founded from St Mary's Abbey, York, by the Benedictines of the latter house who wished to keep the stricter observance.

So it was that about 1930, Dom David came to feel that the monks of Downside were being distracted from their primary task of the *Opus Dei* by the demands of the great public school which they were running. His views influenced many Juniors, including myself, and also four or five of the younger priests. Led by him a number of us formed the desire to make a new foundation with no school.

At about this time it was decided that a new foundation should be made which would have the Junior School attached to it, leaving only the Senior School at Downside. Milton Abbey, a medieval abbey in Dorset, was up for sale and this might have satisfied us as it had all the associations of medieval monasticism including an abbey and part of a medieval monastery. However, this fell through and early in 1933, after looking at a number of other properties, Abbot Chapman decided on Worth which was bitterly opposed by Dom David. Worth was a modern nobleman's mansion, luxuriously appointed and, although in the event it has proved perfectly suitable, it was felt at the time by some that it would be decadent to found a religious house in such surroundings.

Dom David would not accept the decision of the Abbot and Council and he was relieved as Junior Master and sent to Ealing Priory, then a dependent priory of Downside. However, Abbot Chapman agreed that he might go to Rome to discuss his case and he took me with him as *socius* or companion, as I was then ordained and no longer a Junior. Unfortunately we had a wasted journey as, unknown to us, the Abbot was dying. We arrived in Rome on 6th November 1933, to be told that our Abbot had died and that we had to return home.

Dom Bruno Hicks was elected fifth Abbot of Downside on 5th December. Being now a member of the Chapter, I was present for the first time at the election of a new abbot.

Chapter II of the Rule is headed: 'What kind of man the Abbot ought to be' and I quote some extracts: 'An Abbot who is worthy to rule over the monastery ought always to remember what he is called and correspond to his name of superior by his deeds. For he is believed to hold the place of Christ in the monastery, since he is called by His name. Therefore, when anyone receiveth the name of Abbot, he ought to govern his disciples by a two-fold teaching: that is, he should show forth all goodness and holiness by his deeds rather than his words: declaring to the intelligent among his disciples the commandments of the Lord by words; but to the hard-hearted and the simple-minded setting forth the divine precepts by the example of his deeds. Let him make no distinction of persons in the monastery. Let not one be loved more than another, unless he be found to excel in good works or in obedience. Let not one of noble birth be put before him that was formerly a slave, unless other reasonable excuse exist for it. Let the Abbot then show equal love to all, and let the same discipline be imposed upon all according to their deserts. The Abbot ought always to remember what he is, and what he is called, and to know that to whom more is committed, from him more is required; and he must consider how difficult and arduous a task he has undertaken, of ruling souls and adapting himself to many dispositions. Let him so accommodate and suit himself to the character and intelligence of each, winning some by kindness, others by reproof, others by persuasion, that he may not only suffer no loss in the flock committed to him, but may even rejoice in their virtuous increase. And let him know that he who hath undertaken the government of souls, must prepare himself to render an account of them. And whatever may be the number of the brethren under his care, let him be certainly assured that on the Day of Judgement he will have to give an account to the Lord of those souls, as well as of his own. And thus, being ever fearful of the coming inquiry which the Shepherd will make into the state of the flock committed to him, while he is careful on other men's account, he will be solicitous also on his own. And so, while correcting others by his admonitions, he will be himself cured of his own defects.'

While each Benedictine house stands on its own and the Abbot Primate at Rome bears no similarity to the General of a centralised Order such as the Jesuits, houses have tended to form themselves into loose associations termed Congregations, so that we have the English Congregation and the French Congregation which are clearly based on nationality and there are also others such as the Cassinese Congregation which cuts across national boundaries. In the English Congregation the abbots of the various houses elect one of their number Abbot President and he makes Visitations to ensure that the Rule and the Constitutions are being properly kept in each house. He also presides at the elections of abbots.

On the night before the election is to take place, there is the *tractatus* at which names of candidates are submitted by members of the Chapter and the subjects retire in turn while there is a free discussion of each one. This tends to narrow down the number of candidates to at most four or five for the first scrutiny on the following morning.

Before the election, the Abbot President sings a Votive Mass of the Holy Ghost that the monks may be divinely inspired in electing their new abbot. After the Mass the members of the Chapter, that is to say all the solemnly professed monks, proceed to the Chapter House. The Abbot President presides. He first appoints a Secretary to record the proceedings and three Scrutineers to count the votes, and these officials take the oath. Each monk has one vote, but any monk of the house who is unable to attend may appoint another monk as his proxy. He may not stipulate a particular candidate but must leave this to the discretion of his proxy who must cast his proxy vote for the same candidate as the one for whom he himself is voting.

The names of the monks who have been selected at the *tractatus* the previous evening are printed on perforated voting sheets, so that each monk can tear off a voting slip for his chosen candidate and place it in the ballot box. The votes are then counted by the Scrutineers and the result announced by the Abbot President. A two thirds clear majority is required to elect a new abbot; but if after five ballots no decisive vote has been achieved, a straight majority will be accepted. If after the sixth ballot there is still no decision, the final ballot is run off as a straight contest between the two candidates with the greatest number of votes in the previous ballot. Should this result in a draw, the monk who is senior 'in the habit' is chosen; and if both were 'clothed' on the same day, then the eldest is chosen.

As soon as a decisive vote is achieved, the Abbot President asks the chosen candidate if he will accept office and, if so, all proceed immediately to the Abbey Church, singing the *Te Deum* as they go. The Abbot President then instals the new Abbot on his throne and gives him the abbatial cross and ring. Each member of the Community in order of seniority and including the juniors and novices, who have not voted, make their obedience by kneeling at the throne and kissing the new abbot's ring, being then raised up and given the Kiss of Peace. On a suitable date shortly after, the Abbot is duly blessed by the Diocesan Bishop.

Dom Bruno, an Old Gregorian, had entered the monastery on leaving school. He was sent to Cambridge to read History which he later taught. In 1915 he was appointed Bursar, a post he held with distinction until his election as Abbot. During those 19 years, he re-established the Home Farm, installed our own electric power house, enlarged the waterworks, and superintended without a contractor the building of the Nave of the Abbey Church.

Before Dom Bruno's election, all of us who supported Dom David had signed a letter addressed to the new abbot, whoever he might be, asking him to give consideration to our serious spiritual problem, and this letter was lodged with the Prior. The Second-in-Command of a monastery ruled by an abbot is called a Claustral Prior, and takes charge in the absence of the Abbot or on his death until a new Abbot is elected. On the day of his election, Abbot Hicks read our letter and promised to give it consideration; however, he announced a week later that after prayer and consultation he regretted that he could not accede to our desire.

Following this decision, Dom David again asked to go to Rome, and once again took me with him; but this time Abbot Hicks followed us out and took part in the deliberations with the Abbot Primate and Archbishop Caruana of Malta, who came to Rome to assist in any way he could, the latter of course being well known to me from my time in Malta.

First a suggestion was made that the projected foundation should be made in Rhodesia, but Dom David would not agree to this, maintaining that he could not do so without consulting his supporters. The next suggestion was that if an English bishop would invite Abbot Hicks to make a foundation in his diocese, the latter would be pleased to agree. A cable was sent to Madame de Bless, whose son had been a contemporary of Dom David's in the school. She was very influential in the Diocese of Northampton and together with her sister-in-law, Lady Winifred Elwes, whose son was Secretary to the Archbishop of Westminster, they approached the Bishop of Northampton who readily agreed to the proposal. All appeared to have been settled satisfactorily and we returned to England. However on our return the Abbot held a meeting of his Council which rejected the proposal.

At this point it was decided to send a petition directly to the Sacred Congregation for Religious at Rome signed by Dom David and all his supporters. This petition was dealt with expeditiously and the rescript or reply took the form of a very mild reproof stating that the monks concerned should seek their perfection at Downside.

Rome's decision was accepted by us all without reservation and even Dom David accepted it outwardly. He remained at

101

Ealing until 1940 but then left and never returned to the Monastery. His position was regularised later by Abbot Butler who arranged for his exclaustration which meant that he was relieved of his monastic obligation and removed from the jurisdiction of the Abbot of Downside. Thus ended a rather sad episode in which I was involved. Of the others, two transferred to another abbey with no school; and one, my great friend Dom Eric Phillips, became a secular priest and later a Canon of Northampton. Happily, on his retirement, he tried his vocation as a monk once more at Downside and as I write has just made his Solemn Profession.

In relating the episode of Dom David I have gone forward in time. Meanwhile I had received the Subdiaconate, the first of the major Orders, eight days after my Solemn Profession, and the Diaconate on 13th July 1930. Finally on 12th July 1931, I was ordained Priest at Downside by Bishop Butt, a retired bishop who lived in the monastery. I had hoped to be ordained by my dear friend Archbishop Caruana of Malta, who had done so much to foster my vocation, but in the event he was not able to come to England at that time. Dear old Bishop Butt knew this and said very humbly: 'I must be a great disappointment for you!' The following day I said my First Mass in the Lady Chapel.

Sadly, my mother had died in 1926 and did not live to see me ordained. However I had the great happiness that shortly before her death, she expressed interest in Catholicism and I arranged for her to receive instruction from a Jesuit at Farm Street. She was received into the Church six weeks before her death. I had been a novice at the time but was allowed to travel to London for her funeral and burial in Highgate Cemetry. It was perhaps typical of Warwick that he took us all out to dinner at the Savoy that evening.

Warwick and Claire and her husband came to my Ordination, which was very kind of the former as it was not his scene at all. He had resigned from his directorships of the Junior Army and Navy Stores and the Civil Service Co-operative Society and obtained the concession for the Amusement Park at the Wembley Exhibition in 1923 on which the expenditure was nearly half a million pounds. Despite this great success, he suffered very heavy financial losses during the depression in the early thirties and Claire told me later that a week before he died, in August 1935, he placed a £5 note on the table in front of her and said it was his last note. This was not literally true, though typical of Warwick's style, as he then took her to Cowes for the Regatta. He appeared to be in excellent health but died there very suddenly. Sadly I was at the time on my annual summer holiday touring on the Continent and could not be contacted, and as a result was unable to attend his funeral.

The Benedictine motto is *Ora et labora* (Pray and Work) and from my description of the Noviciate the reader will have realised that we did indeed have long periods of prayer interspersed with a good deal of physical work. Every Benedictine house has some activity to keep the monks busy when not at prayer and to support them financially. Some monasteries run extensive farms, others cultivate vineyards and make wine and liqueurs, some make pottery; but right from the time of St Benedict there has been a strong tradition of schools for boys.

Monks such as 'Tusky' Ralph who had entered as graduates were now able to teach in the school, while others who had entered straight from school, such as Wulstan, were sent up to Cambridge after completing their three years in the Noviciate and before being ordained, so that they would be qualified to teach in due course.

I was too old to be sent to university and, as I have admitted earlier, my education had been rather cut short, so I could not be sent into the school right away. Instead I was appointed Guestmaster in 1930, a post which I held until I was sent to Ealing in 1938, and one which I found very congenial and into which I fitted easily through my training as an ADC. I presided at the Guest table in the refectory where I looked after any guests in the monastery. There has always been a great tradition of Benedictine hospitality and, as is well known, travellers in the Middle Ages relied on monasteries for food and shelter in place of hotels and inns.

On the matter of guests, the Holy Rule says: 'Let all guests be received like Christ Himself, for He will say, "I was a stranger and ye took Me in." And let fitting honour be shewn to all, especially to such as are of the household of the faith, and to strangers. When, therefore, a guest is announced, let him be met by the Superior or the brethren, with all due charity. Let the Abbot pour water on the hands of the guests and himself, as well as the whole community, wash their feet. Let special care be taken in the reception of the poor and of strangers, because in them Christ is more truly welcomed. For the very fear men have of the rich procures them honour.'

We no longer get very many casual travellers calling at the monastery but, while the washing of feet, etc, by the Abbot is no longer carried out, the spirit of hospitality remains. It is surprising how many guests there are during the course of the year staying at a great abbey like Downside. For any boy who has been in the school, Downside is his second home always ready to welcome him throughout his life. Some come for peace and tranquillity or perhaps to resolve some crisis in their lives. Others come just to revive old memories and to meet their friends in the Community. Then there are monks from other houses visiting Downside on holiday or retreat or perhaps for some research in the extensive monastic library. Sometimes there are secular priests making retreats in the monastery. But apart from all these, there are visitors from all walks of life who come for many different reasons, including those who may wish to try their vocations.

In September 1935, the Abbey Church was consecrated by Cardinal Seredi, the Prince Primate of Hungary, and raised to the dignity of a Minor Basilica in the presence of numerous prelates and vast numbers of religious and lay people associated with Downside. The junketings went on for a week and entailed much work for the Guestmaster!

In that same year, I started to teach RI and Fourth Form History, which was my own favourite subject, while I continued with my work as Guestmaster.

Meanwhile in the autumn of 1936, the 1st Bn Irish Guards were warned for service in Egypt. Bruce Reford, the newly-appointed Commanding Officer, was very concerned about the moral welfare of the young guardsmen under his command. Many of them were straight over from the country parts of

At Pirbright Camp, 1936

Ireland and would be very lonely in a foreign city where they would be exposed to all the temptations and perils of the Orient. He knew that their deep Catholic faith would be their surest protection and he asked Abbot Hicks if I might come down to Pirbright where the Battalion was preparing for overseas service and preach a Mission. The Abbot willingly agreed and to my pleasant surprise I found myself back at Pirbright Camp once more with my old Regiment. I stayed in the Officers' Mess and I

105

much enjoyed meeting many of my former brother officers. I preached the Mission in a straightforward way, not mincing words about the temptations to which they would be exposed. The word had of course gone round that the young priest was a former Mick, and I think this helped to give them confidence in me and feel that I understood their problems and knew what I was talking about.

It was then that I first met George Stone, who had come over from Ireland to join the Regiment in 1927 and was now a Sergeant Drummer. George was always a deeply religious man and he acted as Sacristan and used to serve my Mass. We were to meet again when I rejoined the Battalion as Chaplain in 1942 by which time he was Company Sergeant Major of Headquarter Company. We soldiered together right through North Africa and Anzio and he served my Mass on numerous occasions. Dom Vincent Cavanagh, one of my fellow monks from Downside, was Chaplain to the Battalion during the early part of the War when they were in Norway. George was then Drum Major and always served his Mass. Vincent told me later about the bombing of the *Chobry* in which the Battalion was embarked. All the senior officers were killed and a fire amidships separated the remaining officers aft from the men forward. Vincent had been having a bath and arrived on deck practically naked to find himself the only officer and virtually in charge. He saw his Sacristan, the Drum Major, and asked what they should do. 'How about the Rosary, father?' replied George, producing the rosary beads which had belonged to his mother in Ireland. Vincent took them and led the Guardsmen in reciting the Rosary while they waited for one of the escorting destroyers to take them off the sinking ship. After the War, George went on to become Garrison Sergeant Major at Headquarters, London District, one of the most senior Warrant Officers in the British Army.

Returning to my story, Adrian Morey was appointed Headmaster of Ealing School in September 1938, and he asked to have me as Housemaster of the boarders in Pickering House, to which the Abbot agreed. Adrian was six years younger than me but two years my senior in the 'cloth' and we got on very well. I have always enjoyed being with young people and I found my work with the Ealing boys very rewarding. In fact Adrian's main complaint was that I kept my boys up all hours of the night yarning in my study.

I am afraid I was not a very good disciplinarian and I was very loathe to wield the cane. I well remember the first time I attempted to cane a boy and the shambles which resulted. Having called the boy to my study and ordered him to bend over, I drew back my cane prior to delivering the first stroke. However, I had omitted to carry out any practice swings before summoning the boy and, as I drew back my arm, I knocked over a standard lamp which in turn knocked over a chair and sent papers flying in all directions. At this point both the boy and I began to laugh, and it became impossible to carry out the sentence.

The Corps was at that time commanded by Major Skinner who was also the School Secretary. In 1939 I attended the Summer Camp at Cheltenham as Chaplain, having by that time rejoined the Army Reserve.

Soon after our arrival at Ealing, Abbot Hicks resigned half way through his eight year term of office. He was a born builder and during his reign as abbot he completed the Sanctuary and High Altar and put in the great East window. He also added the flying buttresses to the Choir and, in 1937, he completed the Abbey Tower and built the East Wing of the School to the plans of Sir Giles Gilbert Scott. He was a very able administrator and we have much for which to be grateful to him; but I think he was perhaps better with bricks and mortar than in dealing with people.

We monks at Ealing journeyed to Downside for the Chapter to elect a new abbot, and on 20th December 1938, Dom Sigebert Trafford was elected sixth Abbot of Downside.

Abbot Trafford was also an Old Gregorian and had entered the monastery straight from the school. He was a very powerful personality and had been Headmaster from 1918 until 1934, during which time he had successfully made Downside into one of the leading Catholic public schools. The story is told – probably apocryphal – that when showing some prospective parents round the school, the lady said: 'Am I correct in thinking that Downside is the Catholic Eton?', to which Dom Sigebert replied, 'No Madam, Eton is the Protestant Downside!' He was an aristocrat and intensely patriotic. As Headmaster, he was renowned for his personal interest in the Corps, and for many

Dom Sigebert Trafford

years took what was then virtually the whole school by special train to London and back in a day to see the Royal Tournament at Olympia. He arranged for the Corps to march from Waterloo to Wellington Barracks for lunch and then travel by bus to Olympia. A first class showman! He was a strong abbot and, as it proved, exactly right for the period of war which lay ahead.

After Ordination, the Constitutions of the English Congregation provided for a month's holiday each year, and during the school summer holidays many of the younger monks journeyed abroad on the Continent.

My friend Eric Phillips who had left Downside and tried his vocation as a secular priest had been sent to the Beda in Rome, and at Easter 1937 I went out to be Assistant Priest at his Ordination in the Lateran by the Cardinal Vicar of Rome. The following day I was Assistant Priest at his First Mass at St George's in Velabro. At about this time, Eric's parents took a holiday cottage at Laugharne on the coast of Carmarthenshire and I spent a very happy holiday there in 1938 and again several times after the War. The author Richard Hughes and his wife were neighbours and friends of the Phillips and we often used to go sailing with them in their yacht. I also met Dylan Thomas who lived in a cottage nearby.

Just before I left Downside in 1938, we suffered a tragedy in the death of one of our boys from pneumonia before the days of antibiotics. Called Stuart Ruys, his father was Dutch and non-Catholic and his mother an Australian Catholic. Very sadly his mother was in Australia visiting her family at the time of her son's death and in those days could not get back in time for the funeral. On the day of the funeral, the boys of the school lined the route from the Infirmary to the Abbey church carrying lighted candles. Mr Ruys, supported by two sisters, walked behind the coffin with the tears streaming down his face. It was a very sad occasion. However, that summer I was in Holland and I made a point of calling on the family who lived in the Hague. The mother was back and I also met a daughter who was at one of the Sacred Heart convents in Holland. I did my best to comfort this bereaved family. The happy sequel is that Mr Ruys was later received into the Church; and the daughter's son, Iain

Stewart, came to Downside after the War where he became a great friend of Dom Wulstan's. When Iain's sister was married in Holland, Wulstan was asked to officiate at the ceremony.

I had resigned from the Reserve of Officers before taking my Simple Vows in 1926. Now in June 1939, with the approach of War, Abbot Trafford allowed me to rejoin the Reserve as a Chaplain 4th Class, with the result that I was called back to the Colours on General Mobilisation and was posted to the 1st Armoured Division at Hereford on 4th September 1939. Thus, contrary to all expectations, after some 14 years I found myself back in the Army.

Chapter 8

The Phoney War

Abbot Trafford, who was very much everyone's idea of an autocratic medieval mitred abbot, had in fact volunteered a considerable number of the younger monks as chaplains, with the result that our schools were depleted of nearly all the young active monks. Poor Adrian had been on holiday in Belgium and, on his recall at the outbreak of War, he found that hardly any of his staff were left at Ealing.

However, as the 'phoney war' progressed, Abbot Trafford decided that he had been a little hasty and wanted to have me back as a Housemaster at Downside. I do not know how he secured the release of a chaplain from the Army in time of War. One story which is no doubt apocryphal but quite within Abbot Trafford's capabilities was that he actually applied directly to the King!

Be that as it may, on 18th January 1940, I was released from the Army and returned to Downside where I took up my duties as Roberts Housemaster. I was kept on the Reserve and I was also appointed a Captain on the General List so that I could command the Downside Officers' Training Corps in place of Colonel Roche-Kelly, a retired officer who had been recalled for some desk job.

As a Housemaster, I came under Dom Christopher Butler who had just been appointed Headmaster; and I got on very well with him. He in turn appointed Dom Edmund Lee, who had been Smythe Housemaster for many years, Deputy Headmaster responsible for discipline and I fear that I must have been an annoyance to Edmund owing to my tendency to absent-mindedness and lack of time-keeping.

I loved the work and I think I was popular with the boys; though I do not know how good I was as a Housemaster as I always found it difficult to be severe. Although a Guardsman, I had no Drill Sergeant with me, and I fear Roberts was far from being subject to Guards discipline!

One of my boys of that time reminded me recently of an occasion when he had asked my permission to go to Bath for the afternoon. This was at a time when Bath was strictly out of bounds. Apparently I replied: 'Yes; but don't get caught by a prefect!' He also reminded me how they used to 'lead me on' talking in my room well after normal bedtime. As they finally crept to bed in the dark, they would suddenly be spot-lighted by the piercing light of a powerful torch held by Dom Edmund, who would exclaim 'Roberts!', disgustedly, and allow them to continue on their way.

At the beginning of term, boys had to hand in all their pocket money and Housemasters handed it out half a crown at a time as required. The issue of money was carried out during the morning break and of course entailed keeping detailed records of all these issues to the various boys. I was never any good at keeping accounts and found this job a dreadful bore so I delegated it to Peter Foden-Pattinson, one of my fags. Peter was first class at this work and, although only a Fourth Former at the time, was absolutely reliable and balanced the books to the penny every term. He would sit in my study all through the morning break each day, issuing the bobs and half crowns. Little did I then think that this was a future Deputy Chairman of Lloyds! The sad end to the story is that when Peter moved up, I appointed a successor whose name I forget, who was totally incompetent and we had a series of disastrous deficiencies.

Peter was one of very many Downside boys whom I recruited for my old Regiment. The Irish Guards was considered to be a Catholic regiment in that the majority of the men were Catholic, though there were of course also Protestants from Ulster. Because of this, the battalion chaplain was always a Catholic priest. It followed therefore that Catholics liked to place their sons in the Regiment; and, although there were Irish Protestant officers including two future Northern Ireland Prime Ministers,

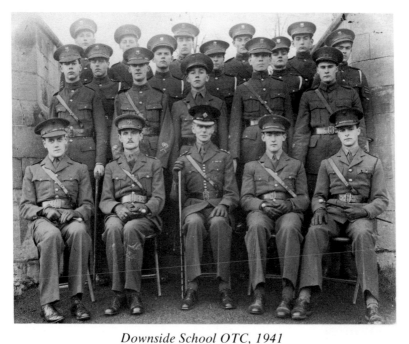

Downside School OTC, 1941
BACK ROW *A. P. C. Bacon, A. P. Stilwell, G. F. Dillon, J. E. Portelly,*
P. A. R. Jordan
3RD ROW *V. R. Medley, P. A. Cuffe*, D. J. Reynolds, A. C. A. Daniel,*
L. R. B. Addington
2ND ROW *D. A. Wheatley*, A. D. Tomlins, M. H. H. MacDermot*,*
D. A. Lambert*, F. Thorneycroft
FRONT ROW *J. K. Maguire*, Mr R. F. Russell, myself,*
M. G. M. Lockett, W. E. Dodd*

Those marked * were subsequently commissioned in the Irish Guards

Lord O'Neill and Major Jim Chichester Clarke (now Lord Moyola), the majority came from Downside, Ampleforth, Stonyhurst and other Catholic schools.

The Regimental Lieutenant Colonel during most of the War was Colonel Sidney FitzGerald, whom I knew well. Despite my brushes with him when he had been my Adjutant, he obviously relied on my recommendations with the result that very large numbers of boys joined the Micks. In fact, I think we may well have held the record for the greatest number of boys from any one school being commissioned into any one regiment. I am glad to say that there is still a steady flow of boys into the Micks from Downside and the other great Catholic schools.

During this time I was also commanding the Corps and had permission to wear my Irish Guards uniform complete with gold-braided blue forage cap which made quite a stir! At that time and indeed until 1968, Corps was compulsory and everyone joined including our many foreign boys: French, Belgian, Polish, Spanish and South American among others. As a result, there was always an element of comedy about the Corps – boys playing at being soldiers. I can recall boys who were so small that when they had fixed bayonets the bayonet rose above the tops of their caps, and when they 'doubled' the bayonet scabbards caught between their legs and tripped them up! Of course in this over-protective age, boys are not allowed bayonets – much too dangerous – but in those days nothing was thought of it, and I cannot remember ever hearing of an accident.

After the Second War when we entered the period of pacificism and 'drop-outs', there came a time when there was much opposition to the Corps at Downside as in other schools which resulted eventually in it becoming a voluntary activity. While good in one way, it must be a lot more difficult to maintain discipline as the boys can resign at the end of any term if they wish and therefore the Officers and NCOs cannot be too strict. In former times, slackness or disobedience was punished with Extra Drills, just as school misdemeanours were and still are punished with the writing of essays. However, in my time quite apart from the threat of punishment, there was a tremendous keenness because of the War and the fact that most of the boys would be going into the Forces on leaving school.

After Dunkirk, my old friend Alex had been promoted to Lieutenant General and was now General Officer Commanding Southern Command. He very kindly agreed to come over from Salisbury to inspect the Corps. The annual General Inspection was normally carried out by a Brigadier or at most by a Major General, so this was a great honour and went off very well.

General Alex was accompanied by two Irish Guards ADCs and the whole party was entertained to luncheon afterwards by Abbot Trafford in style in his private guest dining room.

In 1941, Regimental Sergeant Major Tom Cahill, whom I have mentioned earlier, died of cancer of the throat; and we gave him a full military funeral. The whole school attended in uniform and the Abbot celebrated a Pontifical Requiem Mass. The Corps provided sentries at the four corners of the catafalque resting on their arms reversed. These had to be changed at ten minute intervals throughout the long Mass. Then a bearer party of eight Cadets carried the coffin out of the abbey church and down the lane to the cemetery in the village churchyard, followed by the chief mourners including one of his sons, an Irish Guards sergeant, who also represented the Regiment. At the graveside, a Guard of Honour fired the traditional three volleys of blank cartridge and a drummer sounded Last Post. It was a moving occasion and the boys rose to it, achieving almost professional skill – a fitting tribute to a famous old soldier.

It was impossible to replace Tom on a permanent basis until after the War; but at that time everyone wanted to do their bit and we somehow obtained the services of Regimental Sergeant Major Barnes of the Coldstream Guards – a very old soldier indeed. He was living in retirement at Glastonbury and came over on Tuesday and Friday afternoons by car. He was a bit shaky on his feet but still had a fine word of command. He had a fund of fascinating tales of life in the Brigade years ago and had been Colour Sergeant of the Queen's Guard in the nineties, so he must have been at least seventy five.

About that time a Guards Brigade was stationed in the area and a battalion of the Welsh Guards was at Radstock. We gladly gave them permission to use the Quad for battalion muster parades; and the effect on the school and particularly the Corps was electrifying. We modelled our own parade exactly on theirs, including the Fall In by drum tap and inspection of the non-commissioned officers on a flank before inspection of the rank and file.

In these days of informality it probably no longer happens, but in those days we were punctilious in addressing each other on parade as 'Corporal', 'Sergeant', etc. The boy Sergeant Major at the time was Anthony Wheatley, whose nickname was 'Bean'. On one occasion, I wanted him for some reason and called out to him from some distance: 'Sergeant Major!' but he did not hear me, so I called again without result, and finally in desperation: 'Sergeant Major Bean!' which of course he heard, but the whole parade dissolved into helpless laughter.

It was the advent of the Welsh Guards which produced the revelation that dear old Barnes had been the very first Regimental Sergeant Major of the Welsh Guards when they were formed in 1915, and he was of course fêted in their Sergeants' Mess at Radstock. It is interesting that despite this unique distinction, he still looked upon himself as a Coldstreamer and wore the Coldstream star and buttons rather than the Welsh leek.

As I have mentioned earlier, Abbot Trafford had taken a very keen interest in the Corps when he had been Headmaster in the twenties, and Dom Christopher was a little hesitant about inviting him to have anything to do with it in case he took too active an interest. However, I persuaded him to allow me to invite the Abbot to inspect the Corps in the Summer term; and the latter proved to be well up to his old form. He announced that there would be a prize of strawberries for the best platoon and he proceeded to take a minute interest in every button and belt buckle, taking copious notes as he went along, and inspecting back and front and under the heels! The Corps then marched past in column of platoons and more notes were made. Finally, the Corps was formed into a hollow square round him so that he could address us from the Saluting Base. He went through his notes quite seriously and in some detail, finally awarding the prize to one of the platoons. He then made a typical Trafford announcement that unfortunately his gardener had made a stupid mistake and instead of picking 6lb of strawberries had picked 60lbs and so there would be enough for everybody. The strawberries were then produced from where they had been hidden behind the balustrade of the cricket pavilion which served as the Saluting Base. The whole Corps then grounded arms, sat down and consumed large quantities of strawberries on the spot.

Chapter 9

Back to the Army

In the summer of 1942, Abbot Trafford called me in and told me that he would like me to give up my House and become Novicemaster. As I have explained earlier, a monk takes a vow of obedience to his superiors, so there is no way in which he can refuse a direct order but in practice a superior will normally seek to obtain consent to his proposals. I had no wish to be Novicemaster and I was so upset by this suggestion that I replied, 'Yes Father Abbot, I will do as you say, but only under obedience!' Poor Abbot Trafford was so annoyed at my reply that he roared out: 'Oh very well, get back to the Army!' which was of course exactly what I most wanted; and on 26th August I was posted as Chaplain to the 32nd Guards Brigade.

However, after only two months, on 27th October, I was posted to the 1st Battalion Irish Guards in the 24th Guards Brigade at Sanderstead near Croydon. I was once again serving with my beloved Regiment and with many of my old friends.

Of course the word quickly went round the Battalion that I had been an officer in the 2nd Battalion under Alex in the First War; and one Guardsman was overheard saying to another, 'For God's sake, it's no good going to confession to that fellow, he'd take you for dirty boots!'

Almost immediately the Battalion and the rest of the 24th Guards Brigade were warned for active service overseas and moved to Ayr in Scotland where we were quartered on the racecourse. While we were there changes occurred among the senior officers of the Battalion and, as a result, Lieutenant Colonel Andrew Montagu-Douglas-Scott became Commanding

Officer with Major Michael Gordon-Watson as Second-in-Command. At the same time, Hugh McKinney, the Regimental Sergeant Major, was promoted to Quartermaster. I like to think that Andrew becoming Commanding Officer was the result of a conversation I had with Colonel Sidney FitzGerald, the Regimental Lieutenant Colonel; and this may well have been my single most important contribution to the Battalion's success in action. There is no doubt that under the new team the Battalion was tremendously successful both in North Africa and at Anzio. It was not only a well led but also a very happy Battalion.

Colonel Andrew took up command with the advantage of great popularity, being already well known in the Battalion. As mentioned earlier, I had received him into the Regiment as an ensign while I was Acting Regimental Adjutant in 1925. He only served for a few years and then went on the Reserve and became a successful stockbroker in the City. On the outbreak of War he rejoined the Regiment as a subaltern and served with the 1st Battalion in Norway, firstly as a platoon and then as a company commander. At Sanderstead he became Second-in-Command and before my arrival there had been posted to Sandhurst as the Chief Instructor and later Commandant of the Infantry OCTU. He now returned to us as Commanding Officer in time to take the Battalion on active service once more. He was later to command the 1st Guards Brigade and eventually became an Acting Major General commanding a Division.

He was in fact the ideal Commanding Officer, being very fair and quite unflappable. He was always turned out impeccably and did not believe in unnecessary discomfort, which meant that he ensured that his men always received the best that could be obtained. My great hero, dating from the First War, has always been Alex, but next to him I place Andrew whom I came to love and respect, and I think that the feeling was mutual.

Michael Gordon-Watson who had now joined us as Second-in-Command was also known to me as he had spent 10 years as a boy at Downside between 1923 and 1933, and during his senior years had been one of the boys who served on the High Altar during term time, finishing in the top job of Master of Ceremonies. As I had been a novice or junior during most of his time

Andrew and Alex at Desmond Chichester's wedding

at Downside, we only knew each other slightly; but this was soon to be rectified.

Michael, who had joined the Regiment in 1935 and had also been in the Narvik campaign, was the perfect complement to Colonel Andrew. Whereas the latter was always calm and unflappable, Michael was bursting with energy and enthusiasm and used to rush all over the place getting things done. He was absolutely fearless and always thirsting for battle. Peter Rawlinson, who at that time and right through the North African campaign commanded the Carrier Platoon, told me how, when he was sent back to B Echelon after being slightly wounded during the battle of Recce Ridge, he found Michael who as Second-in-

119

Command had been left out of battle, fulminating at his ill luck and threatening to go and fight with the French rather than sit in an olive grove, whereas Peter was thankful to be temporarily out of it and to be enjoying some degree of comfort and relative safety.

Peter had also been at Downside and only left there in 1938. His uncle was Tris Grayson, who had joined the Regiment by Direct Entry from Cambridge in 1925, a few months before I left the Army. When Tris came down to visit his nephews at Downside he naturally asked to see me, so I had seen quite a lot of Peter and his elder brother. The latter had unsuccessfully tried his vocation as a monk. He subsequently joined the RAF but sadly was killed in the early years of the War.

Hugh McKinney had now become Quartermaster, a very important job and one in which he excelled. He was popular with both officers and men and became a firm friend of mine. However, before this while he was still Regimental Sergeant Major, we had an amusing brush. Although I was Chaplain to 1st Battalion Irish Guards, I also had to look after the Catholics of the other battalions of the Brigade and for this purpose I was provided with a car and a driver who was also my soldier servant. One day the Sergeant Major held a drill parade at which all 'employed men' were ordered to attend. These were the men such as storemen, mess waiters, drivers and soldier servants, whose duties normally exempted them from parade; and it was a tradition in the Brigade of Guards that such men should from time to time be reminded that they were Guardsmen by being chased round the square by the Sergeant Major or one of the Drill Sergeants. Unfortunately, I had arranged to drive over to one of the other battalions that afternoon, so when I found that my driver was on parade I was simply furious. I went straight up to the Sergeant Major on the parade ground and demanded that my man be released. Afterwards Hugh laughingly told me that he never thought I would have the guts to tackle him on parade.

It was about this time that I first met Bill Rooney, who rejoined the Battalion as Senior Drill Sergeant and who was to become a very great friend. Later on Active Service in North Africa and at Anzio we were always together in Battalion

Headquarters and Bill often used to wake me with a cup of tea.

Bill was a country boy, brought up on a farm in County Monaghan, who had come to London to join the Regiment in 1936. He told me how in those days references were required and he had not been accepted by the Regiment until a reference from his Parish Priest had been obtained. His subsequent career and particularly the story of his marriage is so interesting and indeed romantic that I feel it is worth describing briefly.

He arrived at the Depot on St Patrick's Day – surely a good omen – and after the usual four months training, was posted to the 1st Battalion at Chelsea. A few months later, the Battalion sailed for Cairo where it remained for two years. Michael Gordon-Watson, who was then only a subaltern but temporarily commanding his Company, picked him out for a Corporals' Course and he was appointed Lance Corporal. Then in July 1938, there was trouble with the Arabs in Palestine and the Battalion was sent to Nablus for four months to deal with the terrorists. During these operations Bill was Mentioned in Despatches and also won one of four Military Medals awarded to the Battalion. Incidentally it was in this campaign that Michael Gordon-Watson won his first Military Cross.

In November 1938, the Battalion returned to England and Public Duties, first at the Tower and then at Wellington Barracks. War was now in the air; and in order to promote the *Entente Cordiale,* it was decided to send a Guards Detachment to Paris for the Bastille Day Parade on 14th July 1939. There were to be 400 officers and men – 80 from each of the five Regiments. The Adjutant selected 80 men mostly from No 1 Company as being the tallest men; but when they were inspected by Colonel 'Faulks' Faulkner, the Commanding Officer, he insisted that Corporal Rooney MM, be included And so Bill went on what he describes as a most marvellous occasion.

The Guards Detachment was lodged in the Caserne Bessières and taken round all the usual sights of Paris. Then on Bastille Day they marched down the Champs Elysées in eights past a saluting base on which stood the President of the Republic, the French General Staff, all the foreign Military Attachés, and our own General Alex. The Guardsmen were of course in Full Dress uniform and the effect on the Parisiens was unimaginable. After returning to barracks, the men were allowed to walk out; and they cut a great dash wearing their scarlet tunics and forage caps, and swinging their canes. Outside the barracks there were queues of people waiting to take Guardsmen out for a meal or a drink. Bill went out with a pal and on their way back to barracks as they walked down the Champs Elysées they met a French family who stopped to speak to the English soldiers only to find that they were Irish! The Riottes did not speak English; but their fifteen year old daughter, Jacqueline, and her elder brother both spoke quite well. Jacqueline gave Bill her card and asked him to write to her, and thus Bill met his future wife. He did write and they became pen pals right through the early part of the War until the Fall of France, after which he heard no more of her.

Meanwhile the 2nd Battalion was re-formed and there was a great expansion, resulting in Bill's being promoted Lance Sergeant and only three weeks later full Sergeant. He went with the 1st Battalion to Norway; and on its return was posted to the Training Battalion and promoted Colour Sergeant and again three weeks later Company Sergeant Major. He later re-joined the 1st Battalion at Sanderstead as Company Sergeant Major of No 1 Company which was then commanded by Major Basil Eugster, who was to become General Sir Basil Eugster KCB KCVO CBE DSO MC, the present Colonel of the Regiment. Together they won the Company Drill competition; and as a result it was decided that Bill should be made a Drill Sergeant and he was posted to the Commando Depot in Scotland. It was from there that he re-joined us as Senior Drill Sergeant and I first met him. As we shall see, he became Acting Regimental Sergeant Major in North Africa after Ben Peilow was killed and again at Anzio after Jim McLoughlin was wounded.

At Anzio Bill was at one point taken prisoner but somehow managed to 'persuade' his two guards to accompany him back to our lines as *his* prisoners. Later as he came out of the Gullies on what would have been his last tour of duty there, he was wounded and eventually evacuated to Algiers and sent back to England in a hospital ship.

122

After the liberation of Paris by General de Gaulle, Jacqueline wrote to Bill at Wellington Barracks and her letter was forwarded to him at Lingfield where he had been posted as Regimental Sergeant Major of the Training Battalion. She came over to visit him and stayed at an hotel in Lingfield. Jacqueline was now twenty years of age and had blossomed into a young woman; and the following 13th July, the eve of Bastille Day and seven years after their first meeting, they were married in Paris. Hugh McKinney, who was then Quartermaster of the 2nd Battalion, came from Hamburg to be Bill's Best Man. I am delighted to say that they have lived happily ever after, and now have two married daughters and two grandchildren.

On return from their honeymoon, Bill was posted to the Guards Depot as Regimental Sergeant Major 10 years after being a Recruit there. After the War, he again became Regimental Sergeant Major of the 1st Battalion, being with them in that capacity during the Half Centenary Year 1950, when King George VI presented the Shamrock to the Battalion at Chelsea on St Patrick's Day.

In 1952, he was commissioned as Lieutenant and Quartermaster, holding the appointment first with the Battalion and later at the Guards Depot, and finishing as Headquarter Company Commander at Sandhurst, from which post he retired as a Major in 1967. He was then re-employed as a Civil Servant by the Army in the post of GSO3 at London District Headquarters where he served for another 12 years. He finally retired in 1979 and was lunched out on Queen's Guard with General Basil and a number of other very senior officers. There can be few men better known and respected not only in the Regiment but throughout the Household Division.

To return to my story, we were now preparing for embarkation and we received a visit from the Colonel of the Regiment, Field Marshal the Earl of Cavan. Captain Oliver Chesterton laid on a demonstration of street-fighting for the Field Marshal, who took up his position in the Grandstand surrounded by senior officers and by Oliver, who explained the programme. The final *pièce de resistance* was a detonation of some explosive; but unfortunately Oliver's Sergeant had been too enthusiastic with the gelignite, and an enormous hole was blown in the racecourse just by the finishing post and the VIPs in the grandstand were spattered with mud. The explosion also blew out the end of a Nissen hut opposite, revealing a number of Guardsmen, who had not been required and told to keep out of the way, lying on their beds in various stages of undress. We all waited apprehensively for the Field Marshal's reaction; but he merely remarked: 'Typical of the Micks, good old bang to end up with – jolly good show!', as he removed clods of earth from his uniform.

By now we knew we were to sail within a few days, and I remember how I urged all the Catholic soldiers to make their confessions before embarkation. I also arranged for no less than four other priests to assist me in hearing the numerous confessions which resulted from this appeal.

A few days after this we received an informal visit from King George VI. There was strict security and we did not know he was coming. There was no parade or inspection, he merely watched the training. But we knew he had come to wish Godspeed to his Household troops.

On the very last exercise before we sailed, we were dealt a sad blow. A whole platoon accompanied by Regimental Sergeant Major McLoughlin were knocked down by a lorry. Fortunately, no one was killed but there were many injured; and the Sergeant Major suffered a broken ankle and was unable to sail with us, his place being taken by Ben Peilow as Acting Regimental Sergeant Major.

Finally, on 28th February, 1943, we sailed from Greenock in the liner *Strathmore*. We did not know it, but we were in fact destined for North Africa.

Chapter 10

North Africa

We sailed in a convoy of eight ships which took the whole Division and were escorted by a destroyer and two corvettes, though I believe the escort was increased later on. We had an uneventful passage, though there were one or two U-boat scares which were evidently dealt with by our escort.

The men had little to do except write innumerable letters which meant a lot of work for the officers in censoring them. That reminds me of a story about censorship which I heard much later after the War. While soldiers' letters had to be censored by the officers of their Unit, officers' letters were not censored in the Unit but were liable to censorship at Base. A Major General commanding a Division, no less, wrote home to his wife that 'we are soon going to a lovely place where we spent our honeymoon'. The letter was opened at GHQ and the General was relieved of his command. I suppose he reckoned that the enemy would not know where he had spent his honeymoon and he obviously trusted his wife implicitly not to gossip; but of course he had no right to do so and thereby possibly jeopardise men's lives.

Unlike the other officers whose heaviest task was a little censorship, I was very heavily employed in my professional capacity. There is nothing like the prospect of action for concentrating the mind; and this was reflected in the large attendances at my daily Mass and still more by the endless queues for confession. Some put it off to the last moment; but I reckon that by the time we reached Algiers I had shriven a very high proportion of both officers and men!

We arrived at Algiers late in the afternoon of the 9th March in the middle of an air raid and in pouring rain. We disembarked as quickly as possible and then found there was no transport and had the misery of marching 17 miles to a camp outside Algiers where we arrived at 4am and which turned out to be a sea of mud. We remained there in considerable discomfort for three days and then marched back to Algiers and embarked in a very small ship which had been an Irish ferryboat and sailed along the coast to Bone. The transport and motor vehicles went overland, and the reinforcement Company under Captain David Drummond moved to another camp near Algiers. Just before this Company went on parade prior to marching off, I heard Company Sergeant Major Kinnane ask David if he might go to confession, to which David replied: 'Yes certainly, Sergeant Major; but for Heaven's sake make it quick!' David told me later how glad he was that he had said Yes, as the poor man was killed soon afterwards.

As we approached Bone the following day and entered the swept channel through the minefield protecting the harbour, we were attacked by Italian seaplanes with aerial torpedoes, one of which actually passed under our stern – a very narrow escape.

Bone was of considerable interest to me because it is the site of the ancient town of Hippo from which came St Augustine, but unfortunately we did not remain there more than a few days. However, we were there long enough to celebrate St Patrick's Day in style with a splendid parade in the morning taken by our Brigade Commander, Dick Colvin, a Grenadier, who presented the Shamrock; and later by the consumption of large quantities of local red wine. The Guardsmen tended to drink it like beer with disastrous results.

I am sorry to say that we were not very ecumenical in those days and it was the custom that all officers including the Protestants went to Mass on St Patrick's Day. The previous day an Anglican chaplain from Brigade had the temerity to ask Colonel Andrew what arrangements he had made for the non-Catholics in his Regiment. Colonel Andrew was furious and replied, 'I would like you to know that I command a Catholic Regiment and on St Patrick's Day we all go to Mass.' It was fortunate that

Andrew was not a Catholic, as it would otherwise have been very embarrassing.

This is not a military history, but I will just try to give an outline of our situation. As is well known, Operation Torch comprised the landings in North Africa on 8th November 1942. The First Army which landed at Algiers was little more than a Division but it was immediately despatched to seize Tunis some 600 miles away. Within 10 days it had seized the port of Bone and reached Beja only 60 miles from Tunis. From there it continued the advance through Medjez el Bab, literally 'The Gate of the Pass' through the high mountains which protect Tunis from the west; but a little beyond it met the enemy and was driven back onto Medjez and held there. A month later a further unsuccessful attempt was made to break through; and after that it was decided to build up our forces before trying again. During the period while we were building up our forces, the Germans kept attacking our position; but Alex rightly maintained that Medjez was the key to the position and insisted that it must be held at all cost until we were ready to resume the attack.

On 18th March the Brigade moved up to occupy a position in reserve behind Beja. However, half way there we were stopped by a Staff Officer who agitatedly explained that there was an emergency, the Germans were attacking again, and we must go into the line immediately. Eventually our Battalion took over a section of the 'line' facing the Beja-Medjez road opposite a feature which came to be known as Recce Ridge. Battalion HQ was in a farm called Diar el Hammar. The owner had built himself a small villa above the farmyard which fortunately stood on a false crest and thus was not in view of the enemy. Colonel Andrew took it over as his Headquarters Mess and we came to call it the Doll's House.

Battalion HQ was always known as 'White's' after the famous London Club of that name. I had been a member of White's myself before I entered the monastery and Andrew was a member as were a number of other officers. Andrew had brought with him a cook from White's which meant that we always had marvellous food. Whisky was very scarce during the

127

War and even more so in battle zones; but somehow Andrew seemed to have access to an inexhaustible supply, so officers were always finding some excuse to drop into Battalion HQ!

It was about this time that Dennis Madden, the Transport Officer, was ordered by Colonel Andrew to bring up the transport by night. I suppose it was food and ammunition, etc. For some reason there was a difficulty about this and Dennis came to me and said, 'I can't possibly get the transport up tonight. You know Colonel Andrew so well, would you go to him and ask if he minds if it comes up tomorrow night?' Like an idiot, I agreed to do this, went into the Doll's House, woke Andrew up and told him Dennis's problem. Colonel Andrew replied rather testily having been woken from his sleep: 'I have given the Order, for Goodness sake don't wake me up like this', and went back to sleep again. He was of course quite right, and Dennis did get the transport up that night, which shows how important it is for a commander to be firm after making a proper decision. He had the secret of command in that, although he was firm even over quite small things concerning his own comfort which in others might have caused resentment, he somehow did it in such a way that his demands were not resented and he was loved by all.

On one occasion just as we were moving off, he called for a whisky and soda. The Mess Sergeant replied that the Officers' Mess truck was already packed. Andrew simply repeated: 'Sergeant Bates, I want a whisky and soda please,' and that was that. Later at Anzio when we were in the Caves, Sergeant Bates used to bring up the rations at night. One night he forgot to bring up the eggs for Colonel Andrew's breakfast. 'Have you got the eggs?' asked Colonel Andrew. 'No, sir,' replied Sergeant Bates, turning pale. 'Go back at once and get them,' said Andrew, condemning poor Bates to a four hour round trip! Savill Young always maintained that Bates got 'Mentioned in Despatches' for bringing up Andrew's eggs.

At about this time, the enemy became aware of our identity and their Propaganda Unit set up loud hailers across the valley to call out to us: 'What are you Irishmen doing, fighting for Britain?' and many other such messages. The Micks thought it was a great joke.

We now put out a series of night patrols, usually led by a subaltern or sometimes a sergeant, to check the enemy positions and bring back prisoners for questioning. Patrols were bad enough in my day in the First War; but in the Second War there was the added hazard of anti-personnel mines which must have made it a nerve-racking affair for the Patrol Leaders. The first prisoner to be brought in was interrogated by Desmond Fitzgerald, the Intelligence Officer, in the Doll's House. He was an Austrian, very young and rather apprehensive. Desmond, who spoke German, asked him where he came from. When the prisoner replied that he came from Salzburg, Desmond said: 'Oh a wonderful place, I had a holiday there before the War.' This brought tears to the poor prisoner's eyes and after that he was quite willing to reply to all Desmond's questions.

One night Colonel Andrew made a tour of the anti-tank positions, accompanied by Mungo Park, the Adjutant, and a couple of Guardsmen in one of the anti-tank transporters. There was a Standing Patrol on the road in front of No 2 Company; and when the Commanding Officer's party returned down this road, Sergeant Long, the Patrol Leader, who had not been warned, pulled a string of mines across the track and blew them up. Mungo was in the back of the truck with the two Guardsmen and the enormous spare wheel fell on his foot and crushed it. The other two were also badly injured and all three had to be sent home, Desmond Fitzgerald taking over as Adjutant. The Commanding Officer was shaken but fortunately unwounded. Michael Gordon-Watson questioned him closely to ensure that he was not suffering from shock, and Colonel Andrew always maintained afterwards that Michael was hoping to get rid of him so as to take command of the Battalion! I was called in as an umpire and was able to agree that Andrew was fit; but I have no recollection of the doctor being consulted. Of course Michael was an ambitious officer; however he was quite right to enquire, since had Andrew indeed been suffering from delayed shock, he might have made a wrong decision which could well have cost men's lives.

We now come to the attack on Recce Ridge directly in front of our line. One day we were visited by the Corps Commander, the

Divisional Commander, the Brigade Commander and the CRA (Commander of the Divisional Artillery). I had obtained some wine from a nearby monastery which was served to the Generals. What I did not know, as I did not drink wine, was that the jerricans in which I had brought the wine were designated for petrol rather than water, and consequently the wine had a peculiar flavour!

It turned out that what was required was a diversionary attack by a single company on Recce Ridge supported by a vast concentration of artillery fire. No 2 Company under Sam Bucknill was chosen for the attack which went in at first light. Unfortunately, it transpired that the enemy were expecting us and the whole Company was virtually wiped out, only seven men returning after the attack. Sam Bucknill and Tony Rochford were both killed as were many others. The remainder were taken prisoner, many including Colin Lesslie being wounded.

Poor Sam had been married only a few weeks before sailing from Scotland. Bill Rooney had at one time been Sam's Company Sergeant Major and he told me the rather touching story of how, much later, when he returned to England after Anzio he had called on Sam's widow, who had given him her husband's Sam Brown belt, saying: 'Sam used to talk about you so much. I am sure he would have wanted you to have this.'

Despite the terrible loss of an entire Company, Oliver Chesterton was sent back to Algiers to bring up David Drummond and the reinforcements, and the Battalion was brought up to strength again within about 10 days.

Meanwhile another Division had succeeded in capturing Recce Ridge and our whole front was swung round to face east towards Medjez and Tunis, and two Companies occupied a deserted Arab village called Sidi Naceur.

This reminds me of a visit I paid to this village to hear David Drummond's confession. I used to hear confessions walking up and down when we were not in sight of the enemy; and that evening David and I walked up and down among the olive trees while he confessed his sins. He had finished but I had not had time to give him absolution when an enemy plane suddenly appeared and dived straight at us, whereupon priest and peni-

Saying Mass in the Field

tent hastily dropped flat. We were not hit and David helped me up looking rather sheepish. He then said 'Now Father, I would like absolution as quickly as possible!'

I had my portable altar – always known as my box of tricks – and whenever possible I set it up for Mass each day. Mass in an olive grove surrounded by a small congregation of officers and men was for me a moving experience and I think it was equally so for the soldiers. However, my main task continued to be hearing confessions and I made my way round the Company positions as well as I could for this purpose. Long afterwards Bill Rooney told me how he remembered coming back to B Echelon in order to go to confession and afterwards saying to Kenny, the Junior Drill Sergeant: 'I have just been to confession to Father Brookes and he is marvellous.' Apparently Kenny was a hard case with a past, as Bill put it, and he was very shy of making his confession; but after Bill's recommendation he plucked up courage and came to me to be shriven. Contrary to popular belief, Drill Sergeants are made of flesh and blood like other mortals, but I always thought it was very good for the ordinary soldiers to see their officers and even the Drill Sergeants going to confession before battle. After the War I heard an amusing story about Drill Sergeant Kenny when he was at a Recruiting Office which was being inspected by Mr Profumo, the then Secretary of State for War, who apparently asked him: 'Now Sergeant Major, how would I join the Irish Guards?' to which Kenny replied with ready Irish wit: 'We wouldn't touch you, Sir. The "O"s are all in the wrong place!'

Some 10 days later we advanced for what was to be the final offensive to break through the mountains into the Plain of Tunis. This mountain range was called the Bou Aoukaz and the part which we had to attack the Bou Assoud, forever after known as the 'Bou'.

We moved up by night over a distance of about seven miles to our new position. The Companies came up in a long single file and, as it was bright moonlight, the tall Guardsmen cast enormous shadows. I stood on one side watching the men file by and, as so often happens, we were held up at one point for nearly half an hour. I shall always remember how, as I stood there, first one soldier, then another, and then another slipped out of the ranks and knelt in front of me for my blessing before returning quietly to their places. Very many of these brave Irish lads were to die in the battle so soon to come; and for me it was one of the most moving experiences of the whole War, reminding me of what I had heard of the Regiment kneeling to be blessed before battle in 1914.

Easter Sunday, 25th April, was a quiet day and I was able to say Mass and go round the Companies; but that night we attacked and took the preliminary positions from which we were to launch our attack upon the Bou.

The Corps Commander wanted the Brigade to make the attack the following night but there was insufficient time to make the plans and it was agreed that it should be at last light on 27th April. Then the following day the time of attack was brought forward to 1600 hours. I never discovered the reason for this change of plan, which seemed madness without air cover, as it meant attacking across an open plain in broad daylight in full view of the enemy under machine-gun, mortar and artillery fire.

However, at the appointed hour the Battalion stepped off into the open led by No 3 Company. It was now that Guards drill and discipline really told as the men in Open Order advanced steadily into the waist-high cornfields and met a withering fire. There were two olive groves on the line of advance which gave false hope of cover, since they were registered artillery targets. Bill Rooney was advancing with the Regimental Sergeant Major and they both stopped under a tree in the first grove. Bill told me how he had said 'One of us should leave this tree' and Sergeant Major Peilow had told him to go, whereupon he had jumped into a vacated German trench. Almost immediately afterwards a mortar bomb made a direct hit on the tree, entirely demolishing it and Ben Peilow was never seen again.

The carnage was terrible; but fortunately night fell and under cover of darkness our men managed to climb onto the Bou and clear it of the enemy.

It may seem strange that a Chaplain should take prisoners but in fact, although I was unarmed except for my blackthorn stick, some half-dozen young German soldiers surrendered to me.

133

They were rather an embarrassment until I had the bright idea of making them act as stretcher-bearers. I spent the night with the doctor and my prisoners searching for the wounded and dying and giving them the Last Sacraments while the doctor patched them up as best he could before they were taken to the ambulances. Our Carriers were used to ferry ammunition and supplies to the troops on the Bou but could not get up the steep slope so supplies had to be manhandled up to the top. On their return journey the Carriers were able to ferry back the wounded. Owing to the danger of wounded men being run over by tanks, the rule was that they should stick their rifles with the bayonet fixed into the ground beside them. These rifle butts sticking up out of the waist-high corn were a great help in spotting the wounded.

The next day Colonel Andrew brought Battalion HQ back from the Bou to our start position prior to the attack. It was just as well, as our troops on the Bou were cut off by day for the next three days, relief only being possible by night. Battalion HQ was established in a German dugout which had the disadvantage that the entrance faced the enemy. Peter Rawlinson recalls crawling to this opening on his stomach and feeling rather sheepish when he found Colonel Andrew sitting inside calmly drinking a gin and tonic.

At one point, Peter had to take the Brigade Medical team up to the Bou in his Carriers, and they were dive-bombed and had to shelter in a ditch. The RAMC Colonel was livid with rage and shouted, 'What do you think you are doing bringing us up here where we're getting bombed. We are highly skilled doctors!' Peter had to point out that it was necessary to get his team where it was required. Generally speaking, the Germans were very honourable in regard to the wounded and Peter was able to take his Carriers out in daylight to collect wounded under the Red Cross flag which was always respected. Peter was terribly ill with dysentry and it also turned out that he had a duodenal ulcer; but, being in action, he felt that he could not report sick. I stepped in and forced him to do so and thereby may well have saved his life. He was sent back to Algiers and then by Hospital Ship to England. When he recovered he was posted to the Training

Battalion as Adjutant. After the War he became a barrister and a Member of Parliament, finishing up as Attorney General.

Meanwhile the Battalion or what was left of it faced three days and nights of German counter-attacks of the utmost ferocity which they somehow drove off each time. It was during this time on the Bou that Lance Corporal Kenneally won the Victoria Cross for charging down the hill on two separate occasions, firing his Bren gun from the hip and thus breaking up enemy units which were preparing to attack. There were many other acts of gallantry and Colin Kennard, who was awarded the DSO, deserves particular mention among the officers. Many people felt that he also deserved the VC.

Finally the Battalion was relieved from the Bou by the Gordon Highlanders and we were able to watch our Armoured Divisions pour through the gap in the mountains gained by the infantry. A week later, on 7th May, Tunis fell.

I have mentioned the dugout at Battalion HQ and it is sad to relate that when we moved on, Doctor Barnes, our Medical Officer, left some of his equipment behind. He went back to collect this and was killed when the dugout suffered a direct hit. Doctor O'Neill, who had been with the Battalion at Narvik, was appointed in his place. Needless to say, the work of the Doctor and Chaplain complement each other and they tend to be seen often together. O'Neill had the reputation of being an atheist, so when we were seen together some of the more irreverent officers would say: 'Ah, here come God and the Devil!'

On Sunday 9th May I offered Mass attended by a very devout congregation; and afterwards Colonel Andrew read out two messages. The first was from the Divisional Commander congratulating the 24th Guards Brigade on its part in the campaign and singling out the Micks for special praise. The second was from our beloved Alex and read: 'Heartiest congratulations to you and all ranks of the Battalion for your magnificent fight, which has not only added fresh laurels to the illustrious name of the Regiment, but has been of the utmost importance to our whole battle. I am immensely proud of you all: I am very sorry about your losses.'

On 13th May we entered Tunis and were billeted in a large

The King inspects the Guard of Honour with Andrew and Savill

wine farm at Manouba on the outskirts of the city. I had a big airy room which I shared with Savill Young who commanded No 1 Company. The Micks are a marvellous family regiment, the same names recurring down the generations in the case of both officers and men. Savill, whose father had been killed in action with the Regiment in 1917, had joined in 1936 and was a typical example of this family tradition. He told me how when he came down to breakfast on his first morning he had introduced himself to Mr Batts, the Messman, only to be told by the latter that he had at one time been his father's soldier servant and had pushed Savill in his pram! In due course, Savill's own son was to serve with the Regiment.

John FitzGerald, commanding No 2 Company, had been one of many killed on the first day at the Bou during the advance through the cornfields. His brother, George, who had been at the Reinforcement Camp at Phillipville, at once asked Colonel Andrew if he might take over his brother's Company, a request which Andrew gladly granted. I now met George for the first time and had the sad task of describing how his brother had died. I was glad to be able to tell him how Guardsman Crane, John's devoted soldier servant, had carried him for over a mile before himself being killed.

At the Victory Parade through Tunis on 20th May, so many of the top brass were absent for one reason or another that Colonel Andrew headed the 1st Division as Acting Divisional Commander. Drill Sergeant Rooney, who was Acting Regimental Sergeant Major following the death of Ben Peilow, remarked to him that it must be a great honour to march at the head of the Division, to which Andrew replied characteristically: 'Honour be damned, Sergeant Major. I don't want to be marching at the head of the Division. I would rather be marching at the head of the 1st Battalion Irish Guards!'

On the previous Sunday, I had sung a High Mass of Thanksgiving in Carthage Cathedral for the Battalion and the Catholics of the Division. It was a very moving occasion. Afterwards the Archbishop, was entertained by us at Manouba.

There was naturally much relaxation and celebration of the Victory; but one drunken spree ended in an international incident. One night, two Micks, who 'had drink taken', went into the French Officers' Club in Tunis. They were told that they could not come in; but they could not understand French and the French could not understand them. Eventually blows were struck, and not only was a very senior French Staff Officer involved, but the French Commander-in-Chief was present in the Club at the time. It was a colossal 'black' for the Regiment. Desmond Fitzgerald, who was an expert linguist, wrote a letter of apology in French and took it to the General in person. But the latter refused to accept it from him. Finally I went to Alex and asked him to intercede for the Regiment, and peace was eventually restored.

At about this time we were visited by Mr Winston Churchill, for whom we found a Guard of Honour. Colonel Andrew was away and Michael Gordon-Watson was in command. He took post incorrectly on Winston's left as the latter inspected the Guard but was quickly pushed round to the correct side by the old soldier.

We were now employed in numerous guard duties and in absorbing the reinforcements arriving from England which gradually brought us back up to full strength. We had secured a splendid stretch of beach and a bathing chalet which belonged to the Bey of Tunis and both officers and men were able to relax and recuperate after the desperate battle in which they had been engaged.

During this period, King George VI visited Tunis and we found a Guard of Honour for him. The Guard was drawn from No 1 Company, which had the tallest men in the Battalion, and was extremely smartly turned out. Savill Young commanded it; and, after the Royal Salute, His Majesty inspected the Guard accompanied by General Alex, Colonel Andrew and Savill. Tim Keigwin, one of the Subalterns of the Guard, told me how when the cortege had stopped just behind him he had heard Alex say to the King: 'I'm afraid, Sir, it is rather a scratch Guard of Honour as the men have only been out of battle a couple of weeks.' To which His Majesty replied with his usual stammer, as he surveyed the glittering ranks of ramrod straight Guardsmen, 'Sc--rr--atch, my a**e!'

At the end of July Alex flew to Malta and took me with him. I stayed a week and much enjoyed the chance to meet many old friends who had suffered so much during the recently lifted siege of the Island. The people of Malta had certainly lived up to the traditions of their forebears in the Great Siege under the Knights; and their bravery had been uniquely commemorated by the award of the George Cross to the Island.

A great white Cross was erected on top of Hill 212 on the Bou; and a large party including Colonel Andrew, Desmond Fitzgerald and myself returned there to unveil it. Before the

Unveiling the Cross on the Bou

unveiling, I said Mass for the fallen. Then there were the usual three volleys of blank cartridge and the sounding of the Last Post. The memorial is inscribed: 'To the memory of the Officers, Warrant Officers, Non-commissioned Officers and Guardsmen of the 1st Battalion Irish Guards who died on and around this hill. April 27th-30th, 1943. QUIS SEPARABIT?'

At the end of August the Brigade was ordered to the south coast of Cape Bon and we were stationed in a farm at Hammamet – now a popular holiday resort. Soon after we arrived, Alex visited us to make the presentation of the Victoria Cross to Lance Corporal Kennealley. He was accompanied by both the Corps and Divisional Commanders and by two Americans, Lieutenant General Bradley and Major General Lemnitzer. General Alex inspected the whole Battalion and then Kennealley was marched up to him in front of the Battalion by Regimental Sergeant Major McLoughlin to receive his medal. All the newspapers carried a large photograph of Alex, Kennealley and McLoughlin, the latter sporting a splendid black spiked moustache.

After the Parade we entertained the Generals to luncheon. When Alex entered the Mess followed by the others, we all stood up. Alex at once said, 'Sit down, gentlemen, all except that rascally priest', and coming up to me enquired: 'Any complaints, Dolly?'. Everyone was delighted as they all knew I had been one of his subalterns when he commanded the 2nd Battalion in France in 1918. When Omar Bradley was asked what he would like to drink before lunch, he asked for a 'Dark query' *ie* a Daquiri cocktail made of rum and lemon. When this was produced, he said it was the best 'Dark query' he had drunk since he was in his Country Club in Richmond, Virginia, adding 'And boy, could that nigger shake'.

It was at about this time that we had what came to be known as 'Watson's Dinner'. Michael Gordon-Watson had jawed so much about his prowess with the saucepan that Colonel Andrew ordered him to cook a dinner which was to be eaten and judged by himself, Desmond Fitzgerald, Simon Coombe and myself, while Billy Reynolds and Jimmy Quinn were to act as waiters and would be permitted to eat the remains.

The menu was as follows:
  Crème de Tomate
  Omelette Ordinaire
  Specialité de la maison:
  Poulet rôti farci par la queue
  Légumes: Pommes de Terre frites
              Epinards
  Rarebit. Specialité de galle

The judges could award up to 10 points for each of the five courses. Michael was awarded 120 out of a possible 200 points; but in his official report, which was sent home to Regimental Headquarters, Colonel Andrew claimed that this result was chiefly because I had grossly overmarked him and also because Michael's servant, Guardsman O'Shea DCM, had cooked the chicken. Simon added a note that he had had to go afterwards to the Hotel de France in Hammamet to have a proper dinner!

Meanwhile the War was proceeding with the landings first in Sicily and later at Messina and Salerno as we remained in training on Cape Bon. There was a time when we were so hard pressed at Salerno that there had been a demand for two Companies to be sent to reinforce the Coldstream. However with the aplomb which only Colonel Andrew could get away with, he sent a signal to GHQ: 'The Irish Guards are under my command. They joined the Irish Guards to fight with the Irish Guards, and with the Irish Guards only will they serve.' We heard no more of it!

There was a new Brigadier and a lot of rather boring exercises while we were at Hammamet. On one occasion, Savill Young had not read the Exercise Orders very carefully and made rather a mess of it. The Brigadier was very angry and told Colonel Andrew that Savill was incompetent and ought to be sent home. 'Certainly not,' said Andrew. 'Why not?' said the Brigadier. 'Because he's rather a nice chap' replied Andrew. 'You are showing favouritism' responded the Brigadier. To which Andrew replied 'Well, anyone who cannot show favouritism, cannot distinguish between good and bad!' Defeat of Brigadier.

While we were in the farm at Hammamet, we suffered a terrible storm and flood one night which resulted in a fatality.

There was a dry wadhi running past the gate of the farm and a wall of water about 14 feet high came roaring down it from the mountains and into the sea. Late that night Sergeant Maher and a party of men returned from the local town and were dropped by the trucks on the other side of the flood waters. Most of the men decided to wait until the waters had subsided; but Sergeant Maher, who was a very steady and conscientious man, did not want to be late back and attempted to wade through. Sadly he was swept away and presumably drowned as his body was never recovered.

Finally, at the end of November we left Hammamet and embarked at Bizerta for Taranto where we arrived on 7th December. Overlooking the Old Harbour was an enormous statue of a bishop which was at once erroneously taken by the Guardsmen for St Patrick and therefore a good omen.

Celebrating Mass with survivors of the 1st Battalion Irish Guards on hill 212, after the battle of the Bou

Chapter 11

Anzio

We marched through the streets of Taranto to a Transit Camp on the outskirts where we spent the night; and the following day we entrained for a small town, north of Bari, called Canosa d'Apulia where we joined our Advance Party. We occupied a splendid manor house called Monte Garrafa which had its own private chapel. There were numerous granaries all in a filthy state, but these were soon cleaned up and we settled into quite comfortable billets despite the intense cold.

The chapel was also derelict and the door of the tabernacle broken. But a fatigue party soon made the whole place spotless and the Pioneers repaired the tabernacle door. I then went to see the Bishop of Bari, accompanied by Jim Egan and David Drummond. None of us spoke any Italian, so I had to ask in Latin for permission to reserve the Blessed Sacrament in our chapel. I am glad to say that my Latin stood up to this test, and he readily gave his consent.

On Christmas Eve I celebrated Midnight Mass in our chapel which was full to overflowing. I have mentioned George Stone, who had been Company Sergeant Major of Headquarter Company right through the North African campaign and who served my Mass and acted as Sacristan so many times. George had organised a choir when the Battalion had been stationed in Cairo before the War; and he somehow got this choir together again so that we could have a *Missa Cantata*. It was a most happy occasion with many of the men being reminded of Christmases at home.

Hugh McKinney had scoured the surrounding countryside to

find pigs and turkeys; and there was an enormous Christmas Dinner next day with the Warrant Officers and Sergeants waiting upon the men in accordance with Regimental tradition.

The Regimental Band had come out from England on a tour of Italy; and Colonel Andrew managed to have it sent to us at Canosa where it arrived just in time to play at the Sergeants' Mess Dance on New Year's Eve.

Early in the New Year there was a rumour that we were going up the East Coast to join Montgomery; and I recall that Tim Keigwin, a cocky young subaltern, complained to me that the military authorities must be mad to consider attacking against range after range of mountains. I told him to pipe down and that Colonel Andrew knew what he was doing. Within the hour, Andrew sent for Tim and ordered him to proceed across the Appenines to a little town called Gragnano above Castellamare in the Bay of Naples and find billets for the Battalion. Although we did not know it then, we were destined for the landing at Anzio.

Warrant Officers at Canosa, Christmas 1943.
STANDING *CSM's Pestill, Moran, Gilmore, Stewart, Mercer*
SITTING *D/Sgt Kenny, RSM McLoughlin, D/Sgt Rooney, CSM Stone*

146

As is well known, the Germans were fighting a very strong and tenacious rearguard action as the Allies drove them up the Peninsula. A series of mountain ranges formed natural obstacles which greatly assisted the German defences. It was therefore decided to try and outflank them by landing a Force at Anzio only 30 miles south of Rome, and behind the enemy, who were facing our Fifth Army attacking up the West Coast. This Force was intended to cut the German lines of communication and hopefully enable the Fifth Army to join up with it and seize Rome. It was called Operation Shingle.

The Force consisted of the 1st British Division, of which the 24th Guards Brigade was part, and the 3rd American Division together with some British Commandos and American Rangers, and was known as the 6th US Corps under command of the American General Lucas.

The Regimental Band had accompanied us to Gragnano and early in January there was another great party in the Sergeants' Mess at which Bill Rooney conducted an Orchestra from the Regimental Band despite the distinct disapproval of the Director of Music! The Band also gave a concert in the Town Square with excerpts from *Carmen* which were sung by the local population with great gusto.

On 20th January 1944, we were ready to embark at Castellamare and we marched out of Gragnano and down the hill to the harbour behind the Regimental Band to the strains of *St Patrick's Day,* our Regimental Quick March, while Colonel Andrew took the salute as we marched past. The Band then went back up the hill in lorries and brought down the Grenadiers, finally returning to the top a third time in order to bring down the Scots Guards. This gave a tremendous boost to our morale and indeed to that of the whole Brigade as we embarked for action, and it was typical of Andrew's sense of occasion.

Our Brigade was in Reserve and we landed dryshod in the second wave early on 22nd January. The landing had evidently been a complete surprise to the enemy and was entirely unopposed. The orders were first to consolidate the beachhead, second to cut the two main roads going south from Rome to the Fifth Army battlefront and third to join up with the Fifth Army and seize Rome. It was originally intended that a Parachute Force should land by air and cut the two main roads, but for some reason this was abandoned. After the unopposed landing, everyone was jubilant and looking forward to following up our advantage by a swift advance before the enemy had time to bring up his troops. To our consternation we remained disconsolately in some woods all that day and all the following day without receiving any order to advance. It would seem that it had been anticipated that there might be quite strong opposition to our landing; and General 'Daddy' Lucas (as Alex remarked later, 'he was not called "Daddy" for nothing!') was extremely cautious and put altogether too much emphasis on the phase of consolidation with the result that he lost the advantage of surprise and the excellent possibility of a quick advance causing the collapse of the enemy and the seizure of Rome with minimal casualties. Sadly, this was not to be.

Between us and the Alban Hills, a mountain range south of Rome, lay the Pontine Marshes. As the name suggests, it was flat, marshy, open country completely overlooked from the Hills in front. For centuries it had been impassable bog, but one of Mussolini's success stories had been the clearance and draining of the Pontine Marshes, which he had turned into agricultural land. However, the water was still there, as the Guardsmen soon found when they came to dig slit trenches in this marshy terrain.

From Anzio a main road and a railway line run more or less side by side due north towards Rome. These were crossed first by a road on a flyover bridge, which came to be known as 'The Flyover' and secondly by a disused railway on an embankment and bridge which crossed the main road and railway just south of Carroceto Station. These two features and various farm buildings provided the only cover but were overlooked from the hills and were of course registered artillery targets. During the next seven weeks there was to be much bitter fighting up and down this railway line and in and around the features I have just described.

On the 24th January, two days after the landing, the Grenadiers were ordered to send out a patrol along the main road up to the small village of Carroceto. At last on the following morning, we advanced up this road with the Grenadiers leading. They drove the enemy out of the station and village and the Battalion established itself in this area and dug in as best it could. Battalion HQ were set up in a large farm house but Colonel Andrew did not like the look of it and decided to make his Command Post in his car under the railway bridge.

The following day the enemy attacked in force. First with the most enormous artillery barrage including shells from a siege gun mounted on railway track, which we were later told retired into a tunnel after firing each round. They then attacked with massed infantry supported by tanks.

Tony Mainwaring-Burton was wounded when one of our anti-tank guns received a direct hit. Five or six of us, including Michael Gordon-Watson and I, managed to get him onto a door and carried him back to Battalion HQ under the railway bridge, from which he was evacuated by ambulance that night. Tony is 6 ft 5 in and was an absolute dead weight.

Immediately after this the shelling intensified and Michael and I jumped into the nearest slit trench. We lay cramped in this rather shallow trench with Michael's feet round my neck and my feet round his. We just fitted in and lay there for about half an hour with shells bursting all round us. It was very frightening indeed.

I have mentioned how Regimental Sergeant Major McLoughlin had had the misfortune to break his ankle just before sailing from Scotland and so missed the fighting in North Africa. Now on the very first day of the fighting at Anzio he was wounded in the arm and had to be evacuated. Bill Rooney was once again made Acting Regimental Sergeant Major. He later told me how Colonel Andrew had said: 'I am making you Acting Regimental Sergeant Major so that you get the pay. Do not put the badges up in case McLoughlin comes back. If he does within three months you will have to revert.' This was typical of the way Andrew looked after the interests of his men. McLoughlin did not come back, and Bill was wounded in the Gullies shortly before the Battalion was pulled out, but he was later confirmed as Regimental Sergeant Major.

The Regimental History records that it was on this day that I walked up and down the railway track behind the embankment reading my breviary during lulls in the bombardment. This sounds terribly brave and rather like the stories in the First War of Pipe Majors of Highland Regiments marching up and down the parapet playing the bagpipes. Of course it was not like that as I was not in full view of the enemy; but I think the sight of a priest reading his breviary may have been good for the Guardsmen's morale, though I cannot claim that as my intent in doing so. Every priest has the obligation of reading the Divine Office each day, though we were excused this duty under active service conditions. In fact I carried my breviary and my blackthorn everywhere and tried to fit in my 'office' whenever it was at all possible, even if it were in a slit trench. I am sure it had a steadying effect and was good for my own morale!

I have mentioned the intensity of the bombardment and I believe that this day, the 26th January, was the worst I ever spent in either of the two World Wars.

That night we collected as many of the dead Guardsmen as we could. They were wrapped in blankets and Michael Gordon-Watson and I, with Orderly Room Quartermaster Sergeant Kelly and a small party, brought them back to the cemetery in Anzio where we buried them in the dark.

The days that followed saw attacks and counter-attacks; but we never got much beyond the farm known as 'Dung Farm' in front of Carroceto. As far as I was able, I tried to get round the Company positions and of course to succour the wounded awaiting evacuation in the Regimental Aid Post. I carried the Holy Oils and the Blessed Sacrament in a small pyx under my battledress, administering the Last Sacraments and hearing confessions. It is not always realised by laymen that Extreme Unction is to be given to anybody who is gravely ill and not only to those *in extremis*. Receiving the Sacrament does not therefore indicate to the recipient that he is bound to die but only that he is gravely injured; and in such cases the Sacrament is believed to do temporal as well as spiritual good. To underline this fact, Extreme Unction has been re-named recently and is now called the Sacrament of the Sick.

At one time when Battalion HQ were in 'Dung Farm', I

remember paying a visit to David Drummond in his Company HQ in a railwayman's hut. His men were occupying slit trenches round the railway line and the orders were that there was to be no movement during the day and everyone was to stay in their slit trenches. While I was lunching with David off some eggs he had cooked, one solitary mortar bomb fell right into a slit trench occupied by one of his men. The poor man did not appear too badly wounded and the stretcher bearers got him out and back to an ambulance very quickly, while I was on the spot and able to give him the Last Sacraments. Within a quarter of an hour he was back having a blood transfusion; but sadly he died despite the speed with which he had been rescued.

On 12th February we were at last relieved by the Gordon Highlanders and put in reserve to rest for a few days at B Echelon in the woods where we had assembled after the landing. Two days later the Commander-in-Chief visited the Beachhead and the first Unit he came to was the 1st Battalion Irish Guards. The men were delighted to see their hero, General Alex, who walked round the area talking to one and all, often recognising old soldiers who had served under him. It was very early in the morning, the men had not yet shaved and they were utterly exhausted after three weeks of more or less constant fighting. Bill Rooney told me that the General spoke to Guardsman Montgomery DCM, whom Bill described as a very tough soldier, asking him whether he were tired, to which the Guardsman replied: 'No, Sir!' Alex turned to Bill and said, 'You know, Sergeant Major, that's what makes a Guardsman!'

I have spoken of my portable altar which was always known as my box of tricks. Shortly before Alex's visit, it had been hit by a stray shell while I had been up at the front. When Alex heard this, he at once gave orders for a replacement to be sent to me, remarking that 'A Padre without his box of tricks is like a Guardsman without his rifle – no damn use!'

The following day the Germans launched an all out attack in an attempt to break right through to Anzio. Things were clearly desperate and the Battalion was called out of Reserve. It took over a network of deep irrigation trenches to the west of the railway and beyond 'The Flyover' which came to be known as

'The Gullies'. Here the Battalion spent three days and nights in the most hideous conditions of cold and wetness interspersed with constant bitter close-quarter fighting.

Jim Kelly, the Orderly Room Quartermaster Sergeant, had set up a tent for the Orderly Room at B Echelon and here I would offer Mass every morning if possible before going round the Companies at the front. I recall remarking to Jim at this time, 'I think the Battalion has suffered enough', and I decided to go and see Alex. There were two destroyers in the harbour and I remember wondering if I knew either of the Captains. I must have had a premonition because sure enough one of the Captains had been in the school at Downside. He got permission to take me to Naples and back and, having got leave from Colonel Andrew, I set out for Naples and Caserta to see Alex at his Headquarters where I told him of the state to which the Battalion had been reduced. I do not know whether my report made any difference; but very shortly afterwards the Battalion was relieved by the Duke of Wellington's Regiment, which was commanded by that great friend and admirer of the Regiment, Lieutenant Colonel Brian Webb-Carter, whose son David subsequently joined the Regiment and has recently commanded the 1st Battalion.

We returned once more to B Echelon in the woods outside Anzio, where we remained for some 10 days. We were visited by the Divisional Commander, Major General Penney, who said: 'I can't let you go without saying how much I shall miss the Regiment, not only collectively, but individually. It has been a privilege and a sadness to have had your Battalion in the 1st Division during these days, but their achievements, their unfailing response and their willing fighting spirit have been an inspiration. I regret your departure enormously, especially as I fear there is little chance of your rejoining us, but I am glad of the opportunity you will have of refitting and reforming. I wish you well, and I shall never forget what you have done and the sacrifices you have made.'

Finally, on 7th March, we were evacuated to Santa Agatha, on the point just south of Sorrento. Out of 1,080 of all ranks who had gone into Anzio only 267 came back.

We spent several weeks at Santa Agatha slowly recovering. I recall that George Stone, good man that he is, found some starving nuns and managed to get them some rations. We were cheered up by the La Scala Opera Company which for some reason was in St Agatha and gave us a free performance in the Piazza which was much appreciated by Guardsmen and townsfolk alike.

The Regimental Band joined us and, by the time St Patrick's Day arrived, the Battalion was ready to parade for General Alex who came over specially to present the Shamrock and take the march past. The battle of Cassino was in full swing and he had to rush back without even waiting to lunch with the officers. He wrote to Colonel Andrew: 'I do so heartily congratulate you on having such a splendid Battalion. It was a real joy to me to be with them today, and I thought they looked just fine. Smart, proud of themselves – in fact, just what one wishes and expects Guardsmen to look like. It must have impressed all the onlookers very much, like it did me. The Micks were always good (the best in the whole Brigade), but I really believe they were better today than ever they were or ever have been. I am only sorry that I could not remain longer with you – go to High Mass and go round the Company dinners, and then have lunch with you – but as you know I have this important and tricky battle of Cassino in full swing, and it must be won. This is my fifteenth St Patrick's Day on parade with the Regiment and the fifth on active operations – not counting Constantinople and Gibraltar in 1922-24. Good luck to you all.'

Colonel Andrew published the following in Part I Orders the next day: 'The Commander-in-Chief wishes to congratulate the Battalion on their fine bearing on parade. The Commanding Officer wishes all ranks to know that the Commander-in-Chief purposely saluted the Battalion before it saluted him, in order to show his respect and admiration.'

The following night the Officers gave a dance which was patronised by all the Contessas from miles around. On that very night, Vesuvius erupted, and we saw the flames issuing from its crater, and fiery streams of molten lava moving slowly down the mountainside. Next day the lava dust reached us and settled on

St Patrick's Day 1944. Alex presents Michael Gordon-Watson with his third Military Cross, won at Anzio

everything, making food almost inedible. We had to get fatiguemen to sweep the roofs as flat roofs can collapse under the weight of volcanic dust.

During these weeks while we were at St Agatha, Alex invited me to accompany him on a visit to view Monte Cassino. The great abbey founded by St Benedict himself in the 5th century had been bombed by the Allied Air Forces on 15th February. It had been a terrible decision to take. On the one hand the abbey constituted a great natural fortress and, although the Germans claimed that they were not occupying it, there was no guarantee that they would not do so. On the other hand, the abbey was a sanctuary of enormous prestige and antiquity, venerated by the Faithful of all nations on both sides. Furthermore, the Allies looked upon the Germans as the despoilers; but if we were to destroy one of the most famous shrines in Christendom, we should be looked upon as vandals. It would be of enormous propaganda value to Dr Goebbels.

Alex took me in his open staff car with his ADC and we called at General Freyberg's Headquarters on our way to the front. The latter dissuaded us from continuing in so conspicuous a vehicle and provided a Jeep instead. We proceeded to the slopes of Monte Trocchio which faces Monte Cassino and there sat down and ate our packed luncheon. We were in full view of the enemy, though well out of rifle shot, and Alex was wearing his General's red-banded cap and red 'tabs'; but fortunately the enemy OPs did not decide to send any shells our way. As we gazed at the ruined monastery, Alex told me that giving the order to bomb the abbey had been the most difficult decision he had ever had to make, but that he had finally decided that men's lives must come before stones however holy.

The 24th and 201st Guards Brigades were in effect amalgamated and we were nominally transferred to the latter and sent home as there was no hope of sufficient reinforcements to build us up to strength again.

Shortly before we left, Colonel Andrew was promoted to Brigadier and given command of the 28th Infantry Brigade. Andrew was very sad not to be able to bring us home; but he was too fine a commander to be wasted, and he finished the War as an Acting Major General. Meanwhile the Battalion went home under the command of Michael Gordon-Watson.

We sailed from Naples in the *Capetown Castle* on 11th April, and Andrew came to see us off. Just as we had cast off and the great ship was moving away, Company Sergeant Major Paddy Mercer appeared at the quayside. He had been wounded and was recovering in a convalescent home but, when he heard that the Battalion was leaving, he had discharged himself so as to go home with his comrades. Colonel Andrew at once shouted to

Michael Gordon-Watson to stop the ship and pick Paddy up. Michael had a row with the Captain on the bridge. In the event a launch was used and Paddy was duly picked up. This was typical of dear old Andrew. Nothing was too much or too good for his men.

Most of the ship was occupied by American troops and there was an outbreak of suspected smallpox among them. We landed at Liverpool on 22nd April, and returned to Chelsea, being met by Black Fitz on arrival at St Pancras. We were officially in quarantine but, prior to being allowed home, we had the honour to find King's Guard from what was left of the Battalion.

Before we left Italy, Alex had told me to get some leave, promising that in due course he would send for me to return to Italy as Staff Chaplain at his Headquarters.

Chapter 12

Senior Chaplain

After arriving in England and taking some leave, I was posted to Headquarters, 21st Army Group near London. This was just before D-Day and it looked as if I were destined for the war in NW Europe. However, word came through that I was to return to Alex in Italy, the only snag being that I had to find my own way out as every available form of transport was tied up for the invasion. Once again my luck held. I was walking down Whitehall when I ran into the Midshipman who had been in the destroyer which had taken me from Malta to Constantinople so many years before. He was now Captain Robertshaw and when I explained my problem at once offered to help. The following day I received a message at the Guards Club that if I cared to report that night to Naval HQ in Glasgow I might learn something to my advantage. I duly took train to Glasgow and, on reporting to the Headquarters, I was taken on board a battleship which was sailing for North Africa. I cannot recall the name but it was a Flagship and the Admiral very kindly gave me the use of his luxurious cabin for the voyage as he would be using his 'sea cabin'. We arrived on 8th July and a few days later I crossed to Italy. On 27th July I was appointed Staff Chaplain at HQ No 1 District, Central Mediterranean Forces, at Foligno, about 20 miles from Assisi.

It was here that Private Jack Ramsey of the Royal Army Service Corps was detailed to be my driver and subsequently drove me all over Greece, Crete and Palestine, becoming a firm friend in the process. He had been a driver to Father Scanlan in North Africa where we had first met, and he applied to be my driver as he reckoned it would be a 'cushy' billet.

While I was at Foligno, I visited Florence and we called on the Blue Nuns, an English Nursing Order. The English nuns, who had been isolated during the War and had not seen an Englishman for ages, came out to talk to Jack while I was closeted with the Mother Superior. Jack offered to give them a drive round the town and they all piled into the 'pick-up' and drove off. When I emerged with Reverend Mother, there was no sign of them. 'Where's my car?' I exclaimed. To which Reverend Mother replied: 'Where're my nuns?'

On 25th October I was promoted Chaplain to the Forces 3rd Class and soon after appointed Senior Chaplain at Headquarters, Allied Armies Italy, which was situated in Rome. When visiting Rome before the War, I had become friendly with the Maryknoll Fathers, an American Missionary Order who had a pleasant house in the Via Sardegna near the Borghese Gardens. I called on them and they kindly agreed to put us up. Many years later when I was Procurator in Rome, I stayed with the Maryknoll Fathers once again.

When I was posted to Rome, Jack had suggested that perhaps he ought to stay with his RASC unit in which he had many pals; but I was able to tell him that it was due to be split up and the personnel re-posted, so he gladly agreed to remain with me and thus no doubt avoided being sent to Burma!

While in Rome I paid many visits to the Vatican and I saw a lot of the Vatican Pimpernel, Monsignor O'Flaherty, who had done so much to smuggle Allied personnel out of Rome by hiding them in Vatican enclaves like the Abbey of St Paul's-without-the-Walls. He suffered greatly from the cold and we were able to supply him with thick Army vests and pullovers. He was also very fond of English cigarettes which I was able to get for him.

We had the wonderful experience of attending the Papal Midnight Mass that Christmas. Then, on 4th January 1945, I was moved to Supreme Headquarters, Allied Forces, at Caserta. This was Alex's HQ which was housed in the splendid Royal Palace of the former Kings of Sicily. His official residence was in the Royal Hunting Lodge where I often visited him in the evenings or for dinner. Jack and I had lodgings in the town and an office in the Palace, and we spent our time ensuring that all units had chaplains and that they in turn had the facilities they needed. It was a fascinating job and entailed an enormous amount of travel. Harold Macmillan, an ex-Grenadier and the future Prime Minister, was attached to Alex as his Political Adviser. We often saw him driving in his Rolls, and sometimes he was a fellow guest when I dined with Alex.

The War in Europe ended on 8th May and soon afterwards Alex sent for me to accompany him on an official visit to the Holy Father, Pope Pius XII.

Alex had always said that he wanted to take me with him when he called upon the Pope but, when he made his first official visit about a week after the fall of Rome on the 4th June in the previous year, I had not yet returned from England. His ADC at that time had been Captain Sir Rupert Clarke Bt, Irish Guards, who alone accompanied him and told me later how when they had made their adieu the Holy Father had said 'Good-bye, Major Clarke' to which Alex had responded 'He is a Captain', but the Holy Father had persisted 'It will not be long before he is promoted'; and indeed Rupert was made a Major almost immediately afterwards. At the same time, Alex was created Field Marshal backdated to the date of the capture of Rome, and Rupert told me how some Old Etonians on his Staff sent him a telegram congratulating him on celebrating the 4th June (the Eton Founder's Day), knowing very well that Alex had been to Harrow!

Now in June 1945, following the cessation of hostilities, the great Field Marshal made another official visit with a considerable entourage. Besides myself there were Colonel Count de Salis, Irish Guards, Alex's Personal Representative to the Holy Father, Major James Utley, Special Liaison Officer to the Vatican, and Major the Hon Desmond Chichester, Coldstream Guards, who had succeeded Rupert Clarke as Alex's ADC. Alex insisted that I sit next to him in the place of honour in his Staff car, saying 'It's Father Dolly's Day!' When the Commander-in-Chief had been received in audience by the Holy Father, he asked permission to present his Staff, and we were all duly presented to the Pope. Afterwards we had lunch

At the Vatican: Desmond Chichester, Philip Leigh-Smith (Secretary of Legation), myself, Alex, John de Salis, Jim Utley and a Privy Chamberlain

with Sir Noel Charles, the British Ambassador to Italy, and Sir D'Arcy Osborne, the British Minister to the Holy See.

I also accompanied Alex on a formal visit to the Grand Master of the Knights of St John of Jerusalem at their headquarters in Rome at the Palazzo di Malta. Alex was given the 'Cross of Merit' by the Grand Master, which he always wore on his uniform contrary to all the regulations. At his funeral it was carried in procession. As members of his Staff, Desmond Chichester was invited to become a Knight and I was invited to become a Chaplain of Magistral Obedience, which was duly gazetted on 23rd May 1945. Needless to say, I was delighted at the chance to join the Order, as I knew so much about it from my service in Malta. Later when I was back in Malta once again, I was promoted to Conventual Chaplain *ad honorem* on 10th March, 1959.

Alex was immensely popular with the Italians and was cheered as he drove through the streets of Rome. It says a great deal for the magnetism of his character and the aura somehow given out by him that he, the conqueror, should evoke such feelings in these people who were after all the defeated enemy. He and his Staff naturally had many dealings with the civil authorities and it was widely said to his Staff that they loved him so much that they would gladly have him as their King in place of Umberto who had gone into exile. Perhaps in an earlier age this might have happened. He would have done it superbly.

In June I was posted to Headquarters, Land Forces Greece, which was in Athens, but before leaving, Jack and I were both given a farewell luncheon by Alex who kindly gave Jack a signed photograph. Jack recently showed it to me and he had written on the back 'This signed photo was given to me by Field Marshal the Hon Sir Harold Alexander at the Hunting Lodge of the Royal Palace of Caserta when Father Brookes and I were invited to lunch at his HQ before leaving for Greece. JR and JRB 9th June 1945.'

Although we were posted to Athens, we had no Movement Order and had to make our way as best we could. We sailed from Bari on a dreadful old tramp steamer whose captain I bribed with a bottle of whisky to take the car on board. It was so hot that we slept on deck and got covered with soot from the funnel. She called first at Salonika, where I left to travel overland to Athens, leaving Jack to go on by sea with the car to Piraeus.

In Athens we were lucky to find billets with Madame M.E. Tsiropina at 14 Amalias Street near the Royal Palace. She was a delightful old lady who had been a Lady-in-waiting to Princess Selina of Greece. She had been quite willing to billet an officer but was very reluctant to take a private soldier as well. However, I told her how nice Jack was and she eventually agreed and became great friends with him.

While we were in Greece, I had to visit Crete to organise the chaplains on the Island. Unable to take the car, when we landed at Heraklion we went to the big dump of vehicles which had been collected by the Germans when they were in occupation and which had subsequently been taken over by our troops. We selected a very smart Mercedes 2-seater which, it turned out, had belonged to the King of Greece. So we spent a pleasant couple of weeks driving all over the island in considerable style.

On 1st November I was moved on once more, this time to Headquarters, Land Forces Palestine, which was at Jerusalem. We sailed from Piraeus to Alexandria with the car and then drove to Cairo where we spent a few days before setting out for Jerusalem. While in Cairo we met my namesake and fellow Downside monk, Dom Alban Brooks, who was then a Naval Chaplain. It was some 500 miles across the Sinai Desert to Jerusalem; but there were fuel dumps at intervals along the route and we managed to do the journey in a single day. However, at one point we ran into a sandstorm which was most unpleasant. Jack had to punch out the windscreen which was literally 'sand-blasted' and quite opaque.

In Jerusalem we found excellent billets in the German Hospice, where the nuns were renowned for their cooking. I had an office and a Jewish secretary provided for me, which was very convenient. After a time we were joined by the Chief Secretary, Sir John Shaw, who moved there in preference to The Residency because of easier security. This was at the time when the Stern Gang were active, and there was that dreadful incident when a British sergeant was captured by the Gang and hanged in

Myself, Jack Ramsey and Dom Alban Brooks in Cairo, 1945

an orchard, which they booby-trapped, so that when our troops went to cut the sergeant down they were all blown up. Soon after that milk churns filled with dynamite were placed in the basement of the King David Hotel, which was also blown up. The first four floors were used as an hotel, mostly for British officers on leave, while the two top floors had been taken over as Government offices.

Following the Chief Secretary's arrival, security at the Hospice was tightened up, which resulted in trouble with the Guard when it came to opening the gate for my car. I knew the Guard Commander was going to complain to Sir John, so I forestalled him by marching myself in and turning the tables by complaining that I had been hindered in carrying out my duties. All was settled amicably.

163

It could not have been a more ideal posting. For nine months I travelled over the length and breadth of the Holy Land, visiting all the Biblical Shrines and places of pilgrimage, and Transjordan where I met the famous Colonel Glubb Pasha, who commanded the Transjordan Frontier Force. At that time, King Hussein's father was the Emir under British jurisdiction. We also visited Syria and the French possessions in that area.

In July 1946, I lost Jack who returned to England for demobilisation; and on 22nd August I returned myself and went on 'demob' leave. Finally, on 26th November 1946, I was demobilised and returned to Downside, some four years after re-joining the Army in 1942.

With Jack Ramsey, Palestine 1946

Chapter 13

Sergeant Majors and Drill Sergeants

This marked the end of my Army service, although it did not in fact end my career with the Armed Forces. It therefore seems an appropriate point to write a few lines about 'Sergeant Majors whom I have known', as I feel that no Memoirs of life in the Brigade of Guards are complete without a chapter about these great men, who are indeed the backbone of the British Army.

The Sovereign's Parade at Sandhurst at which the son of a very old friend of mine recently passed out into the Irish Guards, was taken by the Prince of Wales. In his address His Royal Highness made the point that, whereas in most Continental Armies their Military Academies are conducted almost entirely by Officers, Sandhurst is unique in the major part taken by Warrant and Non-commissioned Officers, most of whom are hand-picked from the Household Division. It is certainly true that many Academy Sergeant Majors have become household names remembered long after Commandants have faded into oblivion.

I have mentioned that Battalions of Footguards have the privilege of two additional senior Warrant Officers known as Drill Sergeants; and I always thought that these men had by far the most demanding job of all as they took turns of duty on alternate weeks, so that they were in effect on duty for 26 weeks in the year. There were a fair number of sergeants and corporals in each Company to provide the Sergeant-in-waiting and Corporal-in-waiting; but there were only the two Drill Sergeants to provide the Drill Sergeant-in-waiting. When talking to Bill Rooney about this, he said it was accepted as part of the price an ambitious soldier had to pay to reach the coveted post of Regimental Sergeant Major.

I think the great strength of the Brigade of Guards was, and I presume still is, that it is no respecter of persons. At every Battalion Muster Parade all the Non-commissioned Officers are fallen in separately from the men and inspected by the Adjutant before the remainder of the Battalion is inspected. A Sergeant is just as likely to find himself 'in the book' and having to attend Adjutant's Orders the next day as any ordinary Guardsman if he has not turned himself out immaculately. Then there are the 'Young Officers and Corporals Courses' held at frequent intervals. The Young Officers are fallen in with the Corporals and chased round the Square by one of the Drill Sergeants. The Adjutant will be watching and if a Young Officer is idle, he will be awarded a few Extra Picquets. But above all is the fact that with the possible exception of the Regimental Sergeant Major himself, however senior a Non-commissioned Officer may be, he is liable to 'lose his name' for idleness on parade.

When a Battalion of Footguards falls in by drum tap, the men are dressed while the drum rolls, and during this movement the Company Sergeant Majors who are standing in front of their Companies turn and face their men. On the final tap of the drum, the men turn their head and eyes sharply to the front and the Company Sergeant Majors turn about to face the front. The latter is a double movement and as there are only five CSMs, if the pause is not counted correctly, the sound of one heel coming down late is easily heard. I well recall on such an occasion, following the final drum tap, a roar from the Regimental Sergeant Major 'As you were! Company Sergeant Major of No 3 Company. Idle on parade. Take his name!' responded to immediately by the Drill Sergeant. 'Company Sergeant Major Green, sir! Idle on parade, sir!' and out would come his notebook. The luckless Green had literally 'lost his name' in front of the entire Battalion and would no doubt be punished with some extra duties at Adjutant's Orders next day. Does this undermine discipline? Not at all. It underlines that no one is safe and everyone is subject to the same standards and discipline.

Stories of such famous men as Regimental Sergeant Major

'Tibby' Brittain of the Coldstream Guards and Freddy Archer of the Scots Guards (the latter reputed to have placed his own father, an old Bandsman, in close arrest) are legion; but I always thought that Mick Non-commissioned Officers had the edge on the other regiments for their sense of humour and ready wit.

Of course these Warrant Officers knew their own nicknames and the stories which were told about them to the young recruits and they built upon their own reputations. During the Second War, the two Howe brothers were known as the 'Black Bastard' and the 'Ginger Bastard' and there were many tales of these two including the fact that the former had put his brother in close arrest when he was a sergeant and his brother a recruit. Every evening at the Guards Depot the recruits had a 'shining parade' when they had to sit astride their beds polishing their equipment while their Squad Instructor taught them Regimental History and they also had to learn the names of all Commanding Officers, Adjutants, and Warrant Officers of the Depot and of their own Service Battalions. Amongst other pieces of information, they had to learn the name of the Senior Drill Sergeant of the Training Battalion, Drill Sergeant Ben Howe (the Black Bastard). When the Squads of recruits eventually arrived at the Training Battalion and went on parade, a short squat man with a livid yellow face and a black moustache carrying a pace-stick would come up and survey the new squad menacingly without saying anything for a few moments. He would then yell at them at the top of his powerful voice: 'You know who I am, don't yer? I'm the Black Bastard!' The effect on the squad was invariably electrifying. To a man the whole squad would sway backwards on their heels as if they had been struck by some fiery galeforce wind.

My favourite Sergeant Major story concerns an old friend of whom I have already written, Tom Cahill, who was Regimental Sergeant Major of the 1st Battalion from 1916 to 1922. One day when we were stationed at Chelsea in 1919, the whole Battalion was marching down Knightsbridge in column of route and when passing Harrods was held up for a moment by traffic, whereupon a young girl took the opportunity to dart across the road through the gap between two Companies. Above all the noise of the traffic rang out the stentorian voice of Sergeant Major Cahill: 'Young woman, stop! For four years the whole of the Germany Army has tried to break through the ranks of the Irish Guards; and if they couldn't, you can't! Young woman, go home to your mother!'

Chapter 14

Parish Priest

Abbot Trafford's eight-year term of office had expired in September 1946, just before my return from Palestine, and like Winston Churchill, he was not re-elected. As I have said, he was a very strong and forceful Superior, and perhaps like the great War Leader he was more suited to rule the monastery in war than in peacetime. Certainly we owed a great deal to him. As Chairman of the Major Religious Superiors at the beginning of the War, he had persuaded the Government not to call up Novices and Juniors who had not yet been ordained. In return he promised that there would never be a shortage of Catholic Chaplains for the Forces, and he was as good as his word.

On 12th September Christopher Butler was elected seventh Abbot of Downside and he was subsequently twice re-elected, though his third eight-year term was cut short by his appointment in 1965 as Auxiliary Bishop in the Archdiocese of Westminster. He thus ruled Downside for 19 years of great difficulty and interest during all the upheavals of the post-war years and the Second Vatican Council. As is well known, he is a brilliant Latinist and made a great name for himself at the Council which he attended as Abbot President of the English Benedictines and their representative.

Like both Abbot Ramsay and Abbot Chapman, Christopher had been ordained a Deacon in the Anglican Church before he was received into the Catholic Church at Downside in 1928. He taught Classics as a layman in the school for a year and was 'clothed' by Abbot Chapman in 1929, a week after my own Solemn Profession. As we shall see, he probably had a greater

Dom Christopher Butler with Pope Paul VI

influence on my own monastic career than any other abbot under whom I have served. On my return from the Army, he sent me to Bermondsey to take charge of the Downside Settlement.

Like many Public Schools, Downside runs a Club for working class boys, which provides them with sporting facilities. It is funded by Downside and the collection from the boys at High Mass on Sundays also goes to Bermondsey. Apart from the sporting activities, the highlight of the year for the Bermondsey boys is a fortnight in camp at Downside or Worth during the school summer holidays. For boys living in London the chance of a holiday in the country is much enjoyed.

The Settlement had got rather run down during the war years and soon after I took up residence I got in touch with Jack Ramsey and asked if he would like to come and look after me. I promised that if he came and helped me get the place shipshape, I would find him a job. He readily agreed and did a fine job in running repairs. Quite soon after, Vincent Ash, an ex-Mick and a director of the Amalgamated Dental Company, came in and asked if I had any boys who were any use. I told him frankly that I had only just taken over and could not recommend any boy for a job but offered him Jack. Vincent gave Jack a job, and Jack has been with his firm ever since.

After giving up office, Abbot Trafford had a long holiday in Australia and, when he returned in 1948, he took over from me at Bermondsey and Abbot Butler sent me to Beccles in Suffolk as Parish Priest.

I should explain that it is not normal practice for monks to look after parishes. In fact in medieval times when many monasteries were great landlords and held lands away from the monastery, they often employed secular priests to look after their parishes for them. However, this was at a time when there were enormous numbers of clergy available. After Catholic Emancipation in the early part of the last century, when Catholicism started to return to England, the exact opposite was true and there was a great shortage of priests. During penal times a large part of the communities of all the great religious orders had worked on the English mission; and now, when they returned to England from exile on the Continent, they undertook to continue to provide priests to assist the bishops to cater for the needs of the people. Gradually as more secular priests have become available, parishes staffed by religious have been handed back to the diocesan bishop; and now Downside has only a handful of parishes left other than those in the immediate neighbourhood of Downside itself, which are looked after by monks who are able to reside in the monastery.

Being a parish priest was an entirely new experience which I enjoyed and which lasted some five years. The church at Beccles is a very handsome Romanesque one similar in style to Norwich Cathedral and is said to be one of the finest Catholic churches in England. The Presbytery was then a house so large that it has since been turned into a school. It was linked to the church by a Church Hall, so that I was able to get to the church under cover. It was however extremely cold and, as I have always suffered from the cold, this was perhaps the worst penance I endured at Beccles. I had a Curate, Father MacDonald, and we had a Housekeeper to look after us.

The most important Catholic family in the parish were the Todhunters who lived at Gillingham Hall where they had built a church in their own grounds – a little Italianate church in red brick with two campaniles. Mrs Todhunter was our Grande Dame, a delightful person and extremely kind to me. Then there were the Coneys, reputed to be our richest parishioners. Mr Coney had a factory in Lowestoft and was at that time Mayor of Beccles. Another character was a certain old gentleman named Bunbury who had an electric wheelchair the motor of which was always going wrong and causing a commotion in church by emitting loud squeaks. However, the family who became my closest friends were the Traffords who lived at Dunborough.

Cecil Trafford was a brother of Abbot Trafford and of another of our monks, Aidan Trafford. Sadly, Cecil died at the end of 1948 and I did my best to help the bereaved family and especially the young son, John, who was then only 14. Mrs Trafford persuaded me to take John with me on a Continental holiday the following summer and I organised an old friend, Colonel Garnier, a retired Marine who had a car, to take us. In the event I went down with 'polio' shortly before our holiday was due to begin, and I had to arrange for John to meet the Colonel in London and set out without me. It was indeed a strange combination this elderly Colonel and the young Ample-forth boy who did not know each other, setting out on holiday together. Fortunately I had a very mild attack and, feeling so responsible for John, I rose from my sickbed and joined them at Calais. We then drove on through France to Italy; but when we reached Florence, I suffered a relapse. Luckily we were staying with my old friends, the Blue Nuns at Fiesole, and they looked after me wonderfully. John and the Colonel waited a few days and then went on to Camogli on the Mediterranean coast, the next place on our itinerary. I rejoined them there and we eventually made our way back to England; but when I got back I was still not well and had to go to bed once more. Looking back, I realise how lucky I was not to have damaged my health more severely by getting up before I was fully recovered.

John had a friend called Adam Charnaud who was at Downside and whose parents lived in Rhodesia, so he spent his holidays with the Traffords who were friends of his family. These two boys got me into all sorts of trouble. At one time they helped me bag up my Sunday collection money and put only 10 one shilling pieces into bags marked £1 with disastrous effects when I later used these bags to pay the wages! On another occasion when they had their cousins, the de Traffords from Malta, staying with them, they persuaded me to come with them in a boat on the River Waveney in which they were to be pirates with blackened faces and toy weapons. As we sailed down the river, we came across a Quaker prayer meeting on the riverbank, which they proceeded to break up much to my consternation for fear I might be recognised as being the local Catholic PP.

On 27th July 1949, new Colours were presented to the 1st Battalion Irish Guards by HM King George VI in the grounds of Buckingham Palace; and I had the very great honour of being asked to assist at the Blessing of the New Colours.

Michael Gordon-Watson was the Commanding Officer at the time and Tony Mainwaring-Burton the Officer commanding the Escort. One of the Ensigns for the Old Colours was Micky Bowen, who had been in the school at Downside and later became a secular priest. He is now the Archbishop of Southwark. His brother Pat, also an OG, was one of the Ensigns for the New Colours. Their father, John Bowen, had been a great friend of mine and was one of the senior officers killed by the bombs dropped on the *Chobry* at Narvik.

The Right Reverend Monsignor Clarke officiated at the Blessing of the Colours, assisted by Father Casey and myself. After

*The King presenting new Colours to the 1st Battalion at Buckingham
Palace on 27th July 1949*

the Blessing, I had to give a homily which I kept very short.
When the ceremony was over, I was presented to the King, who
congratulated me on my homily being brief and to the point '. . .
not like my people who go meandering on!'

In 1950 the Traffords left Beccles; but in 1952 John accompanied Eric Phillips and myself on a holiday to Lourdes; and
later when I was back in Malta, John visited me there on several
occasions.

In those days, the duties of a country PP were comparatively
light. On Sundays I said Mass at 8am at Beccles, I then went to
Gillingham to say Mass at 9am and returned to Beccles for the
Sung Mass at 11am. There were no Evening Masses let alone
Saturday night 'morrow' Masses, and little fund-raising or social
work. I do not think I would be much good as a modern parish
priest running bingo nights in the Parish Hall!

On 14th March 1953, I ceased to be on the Reserve and was
appointed Honorary Chaplain to the Forces 3rd Class. I thought
this was the end of my military career but it was not to be.

174

Towards the end of that year, Field Marshal Alex, who had returned from being Governor General of Canada and become Minister of Defence, decided that he would like me to go back to Malta, because of the political troubles. There was no vacancy for an Army Chaplain, so it was decided that I should be an RAF Chaplain. Alex knew that I was well acquainted with the Island and a great personal friend of Monsignor Michael Gonzi, the Archbishop, who had been the then Archbishop's Secretary in the twenties when I had been the Governor's ADC. The Governor was Major General Sir Robert Laycock of the Blues; and Alex evidently thought that I could be a useful liaison between the Archbishop in my capacity of monk and personal friend, and the Governor in my capacity of ex-Guardsman!

Alex approached Abbot Butler who agreed to the proposal and I was relieved of my post of Parish Priest. I then had to have a medical examination but, to my consternation, they found an old scar on my lung and this, coupled with my age, caused them to turn me down. I at once decided to see Monsignor O'Connell, the Chief Chaplain; and my friend Eric Phillips kindly drove me up to London. Monsignor O'Connell was not helpful. He saw my rejection as the Will of God and begged me to return humbly to my monastery and give up all thought of the project. However, I knew that Alex wanted me to do this job and I have always made it a rule never to take 'No' for an answer. I therefore telephoned the Ministry and asked to speak to Alex. When they wanted to know who I was, I said: 'Just tell him it's Father Dolly'. I was put through to one of the Secretaries and after a few moments he told me that the Minister would see me at once. Eric drove me round but declined to go in with me and I was shown up to Alex who greeted me warmly and said how delighted he was to know that I was back in the Forces! I then told him the sad news that I had been turned down by the Medical Board; whereupon he exclaimed 'This is nonsense. Weren't you at Anzio with de l'Isle when he won his VC?' Lord de l'Isle was at that time the Secretary of State for Air and I had indeed been with him at Anzio. Alex then proceeded to telephone him at the House of Lords and said that I must be gazetted immediately, that day, which I was! The only stipulation being that I must serve for a year in England before being allowed to go out to Malta if there were no deterioration in my health. I was accordingly posted forthwith as Chaplain to the RAF Apprentice Training School at Halton in January 1954.

Once again I was with young lads and the year at Halton passed quickly. The Officers' Mess had been a house belonging to the Rothschilds and was very beautiful. It was also notorious for having been one of the places where Edward VII had entertained his ladyfriends.

My health proved perfectly satisfactory and in due course on 27th January 1955, I was appointed Senior Chaplain to Air Headquarters, Malta, at Valetta, whither I returned after an absence of some thirty odd years.

Bob Laycock giving prizes at St Edward's College, Malta, when I was Headmaster

Chapter 15

Malta Again

I was of course delighted to be back in Malta, and soon renewed my friendship with many people whom I had not seen for years. In particular it was a great pleasure to meet again my old friend the Archbishop, Monsignor Michael Gonzi, who together with Archbishop Caruana had done so much to foster my vocation long ago. From being Archbishop Caruana's Secretary, Monsignor Gonzi had been appointed Bishop of Gozo just before I left in 1924. He had been translated to the See of Malta in 1943 and had been on the Islands right through the terrible siege of the Second War for which Malta was awarded the George Cross by King George VI. He was himself awarded the KBE in 1946.

There is a rather nice story of Monsignor Gonzi and King George VI when the latter visited Malta in 1943 after Tunis had fallen and the siege had been raised. Malta was the only Colony where Catholicism was the official State religion; and in St John's Cathedral in Valetta this was marked by two thrones: one for the Archbishop and one for the King. When the King was being shown round the Cathedral by the Archbishop, the former was very friendly and anxious to mark his appreciation of the courage shown by the Maltese during the recent siege, and he asked the Archbishop if there were anything which he could do for him. Monsignor Gonzi replied: 'Your majesty, the only thing you can do for me is to sit on that throne' – in other words to become a Catholic, which of course he knew the King could not do.

I was made most welcome by Major General Sir Robert Laycock KCMG CB DSO, the Governor and Commander-

RAF Chaplain, Malta c *1955*

in-Chief. Bob had made his reputation by being Chief of Combined Operations from 1943 until 1947 when he retired from the Army. Although he had been in the Blues (Royal Horse Guards), Bob chose to have a Naval ADC. He reckoned that he could manage the soldiers, but there was such a strong naval presence on the Island that he rightly felt it would be useful to have a Naval ADC who could put him right on naval protocol.

I also met Admiral Sir Guy Grantham GCB CBE DSO, the Commander-in-Chief, Mediterranean Fleet, who was based at Admiralty House in Valetta, when he was not flying his Flag in one of the ships of his Fleet. It was very different from when I had been in Malta in the twenties and the Grand Harbour had been filled with great battleships. The day of the battleship was over; and Sir Guy usually flew his Flag in the cruisers *Sheffield* or *Glasgow* or occasionally in the aircraft carrier *Eagle*. He was to succeed Bob Laycock as Governor and we became very great friends.

Besides the Governor and the Naval C-in-C there were also the GOC Troops and the AOC under whom I came as an RAF Chaplain. On the civil side there were the Lieutenant Governor, Trafford Smith, and the Chief Secretary whose name I cannot recall.

There was much entertaining among all these important officials and very often they kindly included me in their dinner parties. The Admiral had a ship called the *Surprise* which was known as the C-in-C's Despatch Vessel. It was in fact a small yacht in which he could visit the Fleet and, from time to time, he would take his wife and daughters and a few friends with him on a delightful cruise. On several occasions he included me in his party which was most enjoyable.

Mr Dominic Mintoff became Prime Minister soon after I arrived and was of course already a very controversial figure. He had been to the Royal University of Malta where he obtained degrees in Engineering and Architecture and subsequently was nominated by the Archbishop for a Rhodes Scholarship at Oxford. This was strongly supported by the Governor of the time, and he took up his place at Hertford College just before the War. He obtained a degree in Engineering Science and, while at Oxford, met his future wife, Moyra de Vere Bentinck, the niece of an admiral, whom he married in 1947.

After coming down from Oxford, he worked as a Civil Engineer in England until he could return to Malta in 1943 when the siege had been raised. He had been General Secretary of the Malta Labour Party in 1937 before going up to Oxford; and he rejoined the Party in 1944. The following year he became a Member of the Council of Government and in 1947, Deputy Prime Minister. Finally in 1955 he became Prime Minister and Minister of Finance. Mintoff was very much the coming man; and I think that the post-war Colonial Office, which was busy liberating the former British Colonies as fast as it could go, may have felt that Malta was a backward and priest-ridden island that would benefit from the reforming and liberating zeal of a man like Mintoff.

I do not know whether it was a matter of policy but as far as I am aware the only Catholic Governor of Malta has been the Rt

179

Hon Richard More O'Ferrall, an Irish MP and Minister under Lord Melbourne, who was Governor from 1847 to 1851. As I have indicated, all the Governors of Malta whom I have known have been on excellent terms with the Archbishop and the Church in Malta; but it had not always been so.

As readers will recall, I was present in 1921 when Malta received her first self-governing Constitution. Elections were held every three years and Mr Howard's Nationalist Party was defeated in 1927 by Sir Gerald (later Lord) Strickland's Constitutional Party. There followed a serious dispute between Lord Strickland's Government and the ecclesiastical authorities which, prior to the election in 1930, led to a joint Pastoral Letter being issued by Archbishop Caruana of Malta and Bishop Gonzi of Gozo stating that it would be a mortal sin to vote for Lord Strickland's Party. Despite protests by the Colonial Office to the Holy See, the latter upheld the stand taken by the Maltese hierarchy, and as a result the Constitution was suspended for the first time. It was restored in 1932 and, following fresh elections, Sir Ugo Mifsud and his Nationalist Party returned to power. However, this Government soon ran into difficulties over the 'Language Question'.

I should explain that, while Maltese was the common spoken language and English was also widely used, Italian was still the official language of the Law Courts and of the Church, as historically there had been a connection with the Kingdom of the Two Sicilies and until 1831 the Bishops of Malta had been suffragans of the Archbishops of Palermo. Very few Maltese in fact spoke Italian and Lord Strickland with the backing of the Colonial Office had encouraged the study of written Maltese in its place. Finally in 1934 the Colonial Office made Maltese the official language for use in the Law Courts.

However, before this in 1933, the Constitution was again suspended because the Nationalist Government had endeavoured to reverse this policy of encouraging Maltese and restricting the compulsory teaching of Italian in the State schools. Furthermore, this was during the period of Mussolini's rise to power and his agents conducted considerable propaganda in Malta which this pro-Italian policy of the Nationalist

Government appeared to favour. Self-government was not restored until 1947 when the first Labour Government came to power under Sir Paul Boffa.

It will be apparent from the foregoing that, although Archbishop Gonzi came to be on excellent terms with the Governors and the British Government after the War, during the pre-war years when he was Bishop of Gozo, he had been viewed with some suspicion. I believe that I was able to improve the communications between the Governors under whom I served and the Archbishop, and I like to think that in my small way I may have been able to help them see the direction in which Mintoff's policies would lead and that the great devotion of the Maltese people to their Faith was a good thing and not something which ought to be lessened.

Mintoff's wife was a Protestant; and it is ironic that it was she who came to me and asked me to supervise the instruction of their two daughters Ann and Joan in the Catholic Faith prior to making their First Holy Communion at the Mater Boni Consilii Church at Paola on 6th April 1958.

In 1956, the 1st Battalion Irish Guards, which had been stationed at Moascar in the Canal Zone, was one of the last units to leave in the final withdrawal of British troops from Egypt. They sailed from Port Said in the *Lancashire,* an old troopship which was making its last voyage before going to the breaker's yard and, *en route*, called in at Malta. Tony Plummer, who had been a boy at Downside just after the War, was the Adjutant, and I quote from a letter of his which was shown to me some time later. . . 'As we sailed into Grand Harbour at Valetta and dropped anchor, we saw a very smart Royal Air Force launch speeding towards us. In the sternsheets erect as a ramrod stood the very smartest Royal Air Force officer you ever did see. Impeccably dressed in a perfectly cut uniform, with highly polished shoes and wearing a cap at just the right angle with a small peak drooped over the nose in traditional Brigade style, was our own Father Dolly Brookes coming out to greet us.'

Savill Young was the Commanding Officer and I took him and Tony and a party of officers ashore to meet the Governor. Tony told me an amusing story about their departure from

Moascar. Apparently they had marched down to the station and entrained the battalion and Tony was standing on the platform with the Commanding Officer when Savill, who had been with the battalion when it was stationed in Cairo in 1938 and knew the Egyptians of old, became suspicious when he noticed that the engine had not yet been attached although the train was due to depart. When it did arrive, he went past it to look at the front and sure enough it had been decorated with garlands of greenery and a board with Arabic hieroglyphics which were far from complimentary to the Irish Guards! He returned with the Adjutant to the front coach of the train, calling out six men of No 1 Company, the tallest men in the battalion, and ordered them to fix bayonets. He then returned to the engine with this party and declared that the train would not depart until the offending boards had been taken down. At first the driver and his mate demurred; but an order to the Guardsmen to come to the High Port soon sent the enginemen scuttling to remove their notice board.

That summer I was visited by Dom Denis Agius, a Downside monk of Maltese descent who was staying with relatives on the Island. His grandfather had been a Colonel in the Royal Army Ordnance Corps whom I had met in 1921 (see photograph on page 57). I remember escorting the Colonel's daughter, who became Denis's mother, to the Opera in Valetta. One day Denis and I happened to be standing on the Customs House quay watching the Admiral's barge coming alongside filled with all the top NATO commanders. As the dozen or so high-ranking officers marched past us, the whole cortege suddenly came to an abrupt halt as the Chief of Allied Staff barked out: 'Brookes isn't it? We went to Constantinople together in 1922'. It was the Midshipman who had had to take his destroyer out to sea because all the officers were suffering from hangovers. Readers will recall that he had also come to my rescue when I met him by chance in London in 1944 and he arranged for my passage to North Africa. He was now a Vice Admiral and Chief of Allied Staff at the NATO Headquarters in Malta.

Soon after my arrival in Malta there had arisen a problem over the Headmastership of St Edward's College, an establishment outside Valetta, run on the lines of an English public school. It catered for the sons of both English and Maltese people and had been founded in 1929 by Lady Strickland, Lord Strickland's second wife. She was a wealthy woman in her own right, and had also built the Phoenicia Hotel in Valetta on the model of the London Savoy. The first Headmaster was a Monsignor F. Kerr McClement, who had run the school autocratically but well. He was succeeded in 1944 by a Father H.B. Hughes who later changed his surname to Louis. Unfortunately, the latter had become sick; and the Deputy Headmaster, an English layman called Carey, had taken over temporarily. Bob Laycock, who was Chairman of the Board of Governors, was anxious that it should be properly run and wanted to have a Benedictine monk. When I was back at Downside that summer, I discussed the matter with Abbot Butler and it was suggested that Abbot Gleeson, a retired Abbot of Belmont, might be suitable. Abbot Gleeson had been a very successful Headmaster of Belmont, but after his election as abbot, he had suffered a nervous breakdown and had had to resign. He accepted the post at St Edward's and took up office at the beginning of the Michaelmas term. However, he only lasted until the Patronal Feast of St Edward on 13th October which was Prize Day. He made a speech to the parents, after which he suffered another breakdown and had to return to England, and Mr Carey had to take over as Headmaster, on a temporary basis, for the second time.

After this debacle, Bob Laycock asked Abbot Butler if he would allow me to take up the vacant post of Headmaster. Abbot Butler was not very keen as he did not want to put Downside into the position of being responsible for providing a monk for this post in the future. However he was assured that it would not create a precedent and he then agreed to my appointment.

I was very conscious that I had no University degree, and I begged the Governor not to appoint me. I discovered that the School Governors were going to hold a meeting, so I set up a sort of one man picket and pleaded with each Governor as he went in not to vote for me. Nevertheless at the end of the meeting, they told me that I had been appointed and in the event it turned out a success.

On 4th June 1956 I resigned as RAF Chaplain on appointment as Rector and Headmaster of St Edward's; but I was made Honorary RAF Chaplain with the rank of Squadron Leader for life – an appointment which I still hold. This meant that, though I was no longer paid by the Air Force, I could continue my work as chaplain with the airmen on a part-time basis and I was still able to wear RAF Chaplain's uniform.

I now entered upon ten very happy years as Rector of St Edward's College. I have always loved being with boys; and I found my work with these predominantly Maltese boys very rewarding. I have mentioned Mr Carey, who continued as Deputy Headmaster. He was an excellent administrator and marvellous at such things as timetables which were a closed book to me. In many ways he was a very dedicated man, the only unfortunate thing was that he lived with his wife in a flat in the grounds and owing to poor health was unable to do much after school hours. This put rather a burden on me to look after the school at night. I had two Maltese priests, Father William Bailey and Father Anton Mifsud, who taught in the school but left about 6pm. They would hear the boys' confessions before they left, but often boys would want to go to confession at other times and ask me to hear them. It is not of course customary for Headmasters to do this, so I asked Archbishop Gonzi for advice. With true wisdom he said: 'If they come to you, hear them. It would be wrong for you to set yourself up as a confessor, but if the boys make the approach, it would be wrong to refuse.' In the end half the school were coming to me.

I had a number of excellent Head Boys; and one whom I remember well was Victor Custo, who was a real leader. Although there was of course a Duty Master who slept in the school, when I was going out to dinner, Victor would say to me: 'Father, you mustn't worry. I shall be up and about and looking after the school. It doesn't matter how late you are, I shall be looking after the whole school.' . . . and he was as good as his word.

As described earlier in this chapter, the Constitution had been

Prefects of St Edward's College 1963.
BACK ROW R. Duggan, K. Mizzi, R. Chalmers, N. Grima
MIDDLE ROW E. Montanaro, J. Bonello, M. V. Bonavita, A. Mamo,
A. Orhnial, T. E. Cutajar
FRONT ROW N. Degiorgio, V. Custo, myself, J. Hurle-Hobbs,
A. Georgiou

suspended on several occasions and this happened again in
1958. Since becoming Prime Minister in 1955, Mintoff had
proposed a new Constitution based on integration with Great
Britain in which there would be a Maltese Parliament but in
addition there would be three Maltese MPs returned to Westminster. This was approved in principle by the British Government subject to the wishes of the Maltese people. A referendum
was held accordingly in 1956 and 75 per cent of those voting
were in favour; but 40 per cent of the electorate abstained as
both the Nationalists and the Church were opposed to the
referendum. The British Government decided to go ahead with
the new Constitution, but to postpone that part of the plan

185

which called for Maltese MPs in the House of Commons. However the plan also called for very substantial financial aid from Britain because the whole of the Maltese economy depended upon the work provided by the naval dockyard and in supplying the needs of the large garrison. There was very little other industry. The disputes over the amount of financial aid were worsened when it was announced in 1957 that Britain was to run down the Forces by nearly 50 per cent during the next five years and that the brunt of these cuts would fall on the Colonial garrisons. It was apparent that this would seriously affect employment in the Dockyard which was the largest employer in Malta.

In March 1958, Mintoff led a Maltese delegation to discuss financial aid with the Colonial Secretary in London. The negotiations broke down and when Mintoff returned to Malta, he made an emotional speech to his supporters on 6th April, saying that Britain's terms for integration were impossible and that if agreement could not be reached he would demand complete Independence. This resulted in a series of riots and during the next two weeks large numbers of his supporters from the dockyard came into the city every evening and marched up and down Kingsway, the main street, jeering at the Governor and throwing stones at Government buildings and other targets such as the newspaper offices of Mabel Strickland's *Times of Malta,* so that Valetta was like a beseiged city.

Mintoff was now ready to go to the Country with Independence as the main issue of a General Election but, before doing so, he wished to restore good relations with the Church. The Labour Government had antagonised the Church in a number of ways since it had been in power and this had been exacerbated when the Caravaggio paintings, one of the greatest treasures of the Cathedral, which had been sent to Rome for an exhibition, were seized on their return with a view to their being put into a museum. The Caravaggio paintings were now secretly returned to the Cathedral during the night of 17th April, and the Archbishop subsequently announced that good relations with the Government had been resumed. Four days later on 21st April, Mintoff made a broadcast announcing his Government's impending resignation and stating that he and his colleagues no longer wanted to be responsible for public peace and order. Immediately afterwards he tendered his resignation to the Governor but, although refusing to form a caretaker Government, he agreed to remain in office until an alternative Government could be formed.

This sparked off further rioting and Mintoff, who had remained Minister of Police, now tried to use his authority in a most controversial way. He ordered the mounted police to be withdrawn from the city; but fortunately the Commissioner of Police went to the Governor and asked whether he was to accept the Prime Minister's orders in this matter. Bob Laycock told him to disregard the Prime Minister's instructions and keep the police at their posts. The following day Mintoff demanded that the Commissioner of Police be dismissed. When the Governor refused, Mintoff resigned and Bob Laycock took over direct rule himself. The Constitution was subsequently withdrawn by the Colonial Office, and self-government was not restored until 1962.

At the end of 1959, Bob Laycock retired and Admiral Sir Guy Grantham returned to the Island as Governor and Commander-in-Chief. He was the penultimate Governor and it is interesting that the very first Governor was the only other one to have been a Naval Officer. After Napoleon had taken the Island from the Knights in 1798, Nelson invested the Island and left one of his captains, Captain Alexander Ball, in charge of the siege. With the help of the Maltese, the latter managed to drive the French garrison back into Valetta and starve them out. Nelson then installed the gallant Captain as Commissioner and, when things settled down and the Maltese invited us to remain, he was promoted Rear Admiral and appointed the first Governor and Commander-in-Chief. Since that time down to Guy Grantham's appointment the Governors had all been Generals with the exception of one or two civilians.

Just as Bob Laycock had had a sailor as his ADC, Guy Grantham applied to the War Office for a soldier and, from three officers offered to him, he selected Captain Simon Kerr-Smiley of the Cameron Highlanders. Simon was a pleasant young man who was a Catholic and did me the honour of asking me to officiate at his wedding at St Patrick's in Sliema on 15th January 1960, to a charming girl called Jennifer. The reception was a splendid affair at the San Anton Palace.

When Guy retired from the Navy and was offered the job of Governor, Leading Seaman Lawrence, who had been his driver for many years, said 'What about me and Mary?', so Guy persuaded the Admiralty to let him take Lawrence to Malta as his valet. By this time junior officers no longer had individual soldier servants as they had when I had been an ADC, and Simon had no servant. The Admiral used to joke that when there was some big ceremony and they were both putting on their Dress uniforms, Leading Seaman Lawrence had to leave the Admiral to dress himself and look after the ADC whose Highland uniform was so much more complex!

After about eighteen months, the Camerons were sent out to the East on active service and Guy felt he ought to release Simon to rejoin his Regiment. Captain Robin Rising of the Royal Marines was then appointed ADC in his place. Robin was another charming young man and very efficient. He is now retired from the Service and has the pleasant post of Secretary to the Royal Yacht Squadron at Cowes.

Guy Grantham had had a very long connection with Malta during his service in the Navy. He first visited it in 1919 even earlier than me, and remembers the arrival in Valetta of the Dowager Empress of Russia in the battleship *Marlborough*. He was also there as Sublieutenant of a destroyer in 1921 but we did not meet. As he said, he was then far too humble to mix with Governor's ADCs! He was in Malta again in 1933 as a Commander in the Submarine flotilla and got married to his dear wife, Beryl, at that time. Three years later he was back again on the Commander-in-Chief's Staff. He served in the Mediterranean Fleet during the War; and was stationed in Malta in 1947 and again in 1950. Finally, he was Commander-in-Chief, Mediterranean Fleet from 1954 to 1957.

As I have said, we had become good friends during his time as Naval C-in-C and we became even closer after he was appointed Governor. He had of course met Archbishop Gonzi on many

188

Guy Grantham, Grand Harbour, Valetta 1957

occasions socially; but now that he was Governor and particularly as self-government had been suspended and he was concerned in the day to day tasks of direct rule, he had to meet His
Grace very frequently on business affairs as well as socially. He
and the Archbishop came to know and value each other's sterl-
ing qualities and became and still are firm friends. I am honoured that he pays me the compliment of claiming that I was

189

largely responsible for his coming to know the Archbishop so well.

During the school holidays, St Edward's closed down completely, and I lived alone in the school. It was typical of Guy's thoughtfulness that he became aware of this and on several occasions invited me to stay with him and his family at the San Anton Palace which I knew so well from my time as ADC. I spent a very happy Christmas there in 1960 and again in 1961, and also at Easter 1962, just before they finished their tour of duty. In the long Summer Holidays, I returned to England and stayed at Downside and also visited my family and friends.

During my time in Malta many friends came out from England to see me, as Malta is of course a delightful place to spend a holiday. Not only does it enjoy excellent weather but there is so much of historical interest in the island.

My great friend Eric Phillips, by then a Canon of Northampton, came several times. On one occasion he brought his brother to spend a holiday with me, and one day I had arranged a special outing with them, when a Senior Chaplain flew in. I really should have cancelled the outing so as to be with him, but I regret to say that I pleaded a prior engagement and handed him over to another chaplain who was a Franciscan friar. We went off on our outing and in the evening we had dinner at a restaurant on the rocks in St Paul's Bay. To my horror the Franciscan brought the VIP Senior Chaplain, who was an Irishman, to this restaurant while we were halfway through our dinner. Fortunately, we were not in clericals so he did not spot us but Eric wickedly summoned the Head Waiter and asked for the orchestra to play to this guest: 'While Irish eyes are smiling'. The Senior Chaplain was delighted, taking it as a great compliment and little realising that it had been instigated by us truants!

In those days films were very carefully censored before being released in Malta. The chap in charge of the cinemas had a small private screening room in which they ran through the new films in front of the censors and cut out large chunks which were deemed unsuitable for public exhibition. The result was a considerable loss of continuity. The Governor would often have small dinner parties after which he and his guests would go to this cinema which only had 16 seats and see the new films before they had been cut. Although priests are allowed to go to the cinema in England, it was not permitted in Malta; and I naturally had to conform to this rule so as not to give scandal. However, Guy knew this and often included me in these after dinner showings.

In March 1962, it was decided to grant self-government again and a General Election was held. A short time before this a political meeting was arranged in a small village in the square in front of the church. It was to take place on a Sunday afternoon and, as the priest was having a catechism class between 3 and 3.30pm, it was agreed that the meeting would be adjourned for half an hour while the priest held his class. In the event, Mintoff's Labour Party supporters started their meeting and then adjourned for a drink while the priest held his class. At 3.30 the meeting started again but, at the same time the church bells rang out and continued ringing so that no one could be heard. There was an uproar and stones were thrown at the church. Finally, as they could not continue the meeting, the Commissioner of Police told the crowd to disperse. Guy was very angry about this as Mintoff's people had stuck to their part of the bargain and the Parish Priest had been highly provocative. The next day, after receiving a full report from the Commissioner of Police, Guy asked the Archbishop to come and see him. When the latter arrived, he agreed that he had heard of the incident; whereupon Guy suggested that they send for the offending priest forthwith and his ADC was despatched to collect him. On his arrival, Guy said: 'Your Grace, I am now going to tell you the full story of what occurred.' After he had finished the Parish Priest tried to excuse himself by saying that it was not his fault and that he could not restrain his congregation. The Governor then said: 'You're the man in charge of the Church and the Parish, and it was your duty to take charge and prevent this happening; and I am disgusted that you failed to do so.' The Archbishop added 'I entirely agree with the Governor. Get out!' This illustrates how perfectly in tune with each other these two men were. They were both men of action, used to making decisions and to giving commands and expecting them to be obeyed. They would not tolerate failure in carrying out one's duty.

Shortly before the election, Mintoff came to the Governor and objected to some of the Electoral Commissioners whose job it was to supervise the elections and prevent intimidation. He wanted half of them to be chosen from his supporters. Guy replied that the Commissioners had been specially chosen for their neutrality. They were people who had no interest in politics. However, if Mintoff objected to any of them, the Governor had a list of reserves and if he thought the objection justified he would substitute one of the reserves. Mintoff went away and returned later to say that he was satisfied.

At the General Election, the Nationalist Party got the majority and Mintoff failed to get in.

In June the Granthams left the Island which was sad for me as we had become such good friends. On the last day before he left, Guy said to me: 'There is something I want to ask you before I leave.' Later, as he was about to depart, I reminded him of this remark. He drew me to one side and told me that he had put me up for the OBE and would I be willing to accept it if it were awarded. Naturally, I replied that I would be greatly honoured, and in due course I became an Officer of the Most Excellent Order of the British Empire.

Guy was succeeded by the very last Governor and Commander-in-Chief of Malta, who was Sir Maurice Dorman GCMG GCVO, not a soldier or sailor but a Colonial Service Officer. He had been in Malta before in 1945 when he was an assistant to the Lieutenant Governor. The Lieutenant Governor and the few other British Officers in the Maltese Administration were either members of the Overseas Civil Service or Colonial Office men; but the office of Lieutenant Governor which had existed for a good many years was abolished by Guy Grantham who thought it was no longer necessary to retain this post and relied on the Chief Secretary alone.

As a matter of policy, Maurice had nobody on his Staff who was not Maltese, and he drew his ADCs from the Royal Malta Artillery. Governors who were admirals or generals wore their service uniforms; but civilian Governors wore the Colonial uniform which dated from another era. Maurice looked rather splendid in his blue tail-coated uniform complete with cocked hat and feathers.

He and Lady Dorman were very friendly to me and continued the custom started by the Granthams of inviting me to spend Christmas with their family at San Anton, which I very much enjoyed. I have mentioned the Verdala Palace where the Court used to reside in summer. This custom had long since been discontinued and the Palace had become very run down. However the Dormans re-furnished it so that they could give luncheon parties and hold charity balls, though they never resided there. On Boxing Day in place of the traditional English Boxing Day Meet, they invited all their friends quite unofficially by word of mouth to bring their own picnic lunch to Verdala and the Dormans provided rum punch. Afterwards there was mixed hockey with the Governor in one goal and the GOC in the other! I was sometimes persuaded to take part.

As so often happens, the ADC married the Governor's daughter, Elisabeth. In this case not the Governor's ADC but that of the GOC, Major General Lord Thurlow. George Latham was in the Queen's Own Highlanders (an amalgamation of the Camerons and the Seaforths) and he and Elisabeth made a handsome couple. They had a splendid wedding; and it was quite an historic event because it was celebrated in the Anglican Cathedral and for the first time Archbishop Gonzi attended and said a prayer. This caused quite a sensation in Catholic Malta; and was of course part of the growing ecumenical movement. There is also an amusing story about the wedding. At that time the NATO C-in-C Mediterranean was for the first time an Italian, and he was of course invited. The Governor had read the Lesson which was the well known one on Love from I Corinthians 13, and at the reception afterwards the Italian admiral remarked to Lady Dorman: 'I did not understand why Sir Maurice had to get up and make a speech during the service – mind you it was a very good one.'

Maurice had served in Africa in various parts of the old Empire and, immediately prior to returning to Malta as Governor, he had been in Sierra Leone. He had gone there as last Governor and Commander-in-Chief in 1956 and after Independence in 1961 became their first Governor General. Now he was to repeat the operation. In 1964, two years after his arrival, Malta was granted complete Independence with Dominion status and Maurice became the first Governor General and the last Englishman to hold that post. He thus had the unique distinction of presiding over the Independence of two countries whose association with Britain went back well over 150 years.

The Duke of Edinburgh came out for the Independence Day celebrations, which was a great compliment to Malta, as all the other Colonies granted independence had only been honoured by other members of the Royal Family. The Queen never presided over Independence celebrations, so to send her Consort was the next best thing, and reflected her great affection for the Island and its people which dated back to the happy times she had spent there as the young wife of a naval officer.

Giorgio Borg Olivier, Archbishop Michael Gonzi and Maurice Dorman

194

Independence was marked by a big parade of troops on the Parade Ground at Floriana just outside Valetta, attended by the Prince, the Governor, the Prime Minister, Dr Giorgio Borg Olivier, the GOC, etc. Mintoff was in Opposition and did not attend. The massed bands beat Tattoo and then on the stroke of midnight the British flag was hauled down for the last time and the Maltese flag hoisted in its place. The following day there was a ceremony in the Legislative Assembly when the Constitution was handed over to the Prime Minister by Prince Philip.

Mintoff and his Labour Party never recognised this as Independence Day as they claimed that it was not until the British and NATO forces had left that Malta was truly independent.

At one time it was hoped that Independence Day might be fixed on the 8th September which was the day the Great Siege ended and also the day on which it was reckoned that the second siege was raised in 1942 when the American tanker *Ohio* came into Grand Harbour with two destroyers lashed on either side to keep her afloat and bearing the vital aviation fuel for the air defences.

At Independence the Nationalist Government negotiated an Agreement providing for the retention of British Forces in Malta to assist the economy of the Island which was not then strong enough to do without it. In fact the economy was still not strong enough after Mintoff came to power and it was not until a considerable time afterwards that the troops were finally withdrawn.

As Governor General, Maurice was not involved in politics; but there was one occasion when he spoke from his heart. The British Government was supposed to consult the Maltese about any reduction in the Forces, but on this occasion such a reduction was announced virtually as a *fait accompli*. Each year at Candlemas, the 2nd February, there was an ancient custom that all the Maltese Parish Priests presented candles to the Temporal Power, formerly the Grand Master of the Knights, now the Governor General. Maurice took the opportunity to speak out at the Candlemas ceremony. He said that he did not think the reduction was right from the point of view of the Maltese people and that he stood foursquare behind them. This might have been construed as acting against British interests; but this was not his concern, it was that of the High Commissioner, the representative of the British Government. As Governor General, Maurice held that he was the representative of the Queen of Malta as differentiated from the Queen of England.

In the 1966 election Borg Olivier and his Nationalist Party got in again, but in 1971 after I had left the Island, Mintoff and his Labour Party finally got in with a majority of only one seat, and that was won by only five votes. Mintoff has been Prime Minister ever since; and one of his first acts was to have Maurice recalled and Sir Anthony Mamo, who had been Chief Justice, appointed the first Maltese Governor General.

By 1966 I had been 11 years in Malta and 10 years in the post of Headmaster of St Edward's. It happened that the Abbot Procurator of the English Benedictines resident in Rome had died and the post was vacant. Abbot Butler was Abbot President of the English Benedictines and therefore very influential in deciding who should be appointed to the vacant post. He obviously looked ahead and saw that I could not continue as Headmaster for many more years and had to consider what work I should do after retiring from the headmastership. I am infinitely grateful to him for his wisdom in deciding that it was in my best interests to give up the job which I loved and take on the new post in Rome for which he considered I should be very suited. I discovered later that he consulted my dear friend, Eric Phillips, who at once agreed that a posting to Rome would suit me admirably. I have no doubt that he rightly suspected that my vanity would be tickled by the honour of the rank of abbot which then went with the job.

At the time, I was very sad at the prospect of leaving Malta and my boys; and even the prospect of being an abbot did not make up for that. However, I accepted the honour conferred on me; and it was indeed very lucky that I left when I did, as a few years later when Mintoff came to power he brought in an edict that the Headmaster must be Maltese.

I have said earlier that of all my religious superiors, Abbot Christopher Butler has perhaps done more for me than any other. When Alex wanted me to go out to Malta, he agreed to allow me to do so, when he might quite reasonably have objected to a monk going off as a chaplain in peacetime. Later when Bob Laycock wanted me to take on the Headmastership of St Edward's, he might have demurred but did not do so. Finally, by his kindness and foresight, he took me away from Malta at just the right time and put me into a post which was to provide me with another 10 years of useful and interesting work. I am most grateful to him.

After one term, during which Mr Carey once again held the fort on a temporary basis, I was succeeded by an Assumptionist priest who had been Headmaster of a school in England. He remained for four years until he was recalled in 1971 to become Provincial of his Order. I believe there were then one or two short tenures but, in 1975, one of my Maltese lay masters, Antoine Cachia-Caruana, who had been Senior Mathematics master and also ran the Sports, took over as Headmaster and was first class. He had been a boy in the school himself and a master since 1949. I am happy to say that he is still in the post, and I understand that the school is very well thought of. In 1979, there was a week's celebration of the school's Golden Jubilee and all the previous Headmasters were invited to attend. Sadly, I was unable to go to Malta at that time.

At Easter 1966, I was struck down with acute appendicitis and was carried off to the Hospital run by the Blue Nuns, the same Order as my old friends at Florence. It was an absolutely first class hospital and I quickly recovered from my operation. It is sad to think that these good nuns have since been driven out. Although some were Maltese, there were also a substantial number of English and Irish nuns and the latters' work permits were not renewed, after which they were ordered to leave.

I finished at the end of the Summer term and was very touched by the evident affection of the boys and their sorrow at my impending departure. The boys knew that I was to become an abbot, and at the end of term they presented me with a pectoral cross. It is a gold cross with a small platinum Maltese Cross on the centre of one side. On the back is inscribed: 'To Abbot Brookes, whose friendship has meant so much to us, from the boys of St Edward's, Malta 5th July, 1966.' To me it is

197

the greatest tribute any Headmaster could have received. I have another pectoral cross given me by the monastery at Downside which has a relic of the True Cross and was given to the Order by Catherine of Braganza, Charles II's Queen, at the time when we were serving the Queen's chapel in Somerset House. I very seldom wear it. I am proud to wear the simple cross given me by my boys of St Edward's.

Perhaps an equally touching moment was when I went to take leave of the Archbishop, dear Michael Gonzi, whom I had known for so many years. He knew of course of my appointment as Abbot Procurator in Rome and, when I was about to depart, he drew the episcopal ring from his own finger and placed it on mine to be my abbatial ring. I have worn it ever since.

Chapter 16

Rome

As I have mentioned earlier, each Benedictine house is an independent unit, but over the centuries, they have tended to join together loosely in Congregations, the English Congregation in fact being the oldest and therefore the most senior. The Congregation is presided over by the Abbot President who is elected from amongst the reigning abbots of the houses of the Congregation.

The Abbot Procurator in Curia is the representative or ambassador of the Congregation to the Holy See in Rome. He is sometimes a retired abbot, that is to say one who has reigned over one of the abbeys but has not been re-elected on the expiry of his eight year term of office. However, if an ordinary monk is selected for the post, he is sometimes given the honorary rank of abbot, as this is undoubtedly very helpful to him in carrying out his duties in Rome. This is because in Rome ordinary priests are numbered in their thousands while even bishops are numbered in their hundreds. Abbots rank with bishops and receive a 'Present Arms' from the Swiss Guard at the Vatican. Apart from this pleasant honour, the abbatial rank certainly helps to open bureaucratic doors in the numerous offices of the Roman Curia which govern the Universal Church.

I was appointed Titular Abbot of Sherborne; and I should perhaps write a word about these honorary titles. Before the Reformation, England was covered with Benedictine abbeys and because this country had been evangelised by the Benedictines we had the unique distinction that many of our cathedrals had monastic chapters, that is to say that instead of the usual

Chapter of Canons the cathedral was run by a monastery attached to it. Instead of a Dean there was a Cathedral Prior with very similar duties and privileges. Examples are Canterbury, Winchester and Durham. The title of Titular Abbot or Cathedral Prior carries no jurisdiction, only honour and precedence; and these titles are conferred as a mark of honour on senior monks. Certain titles are associated with particular houses, so that a monk of Ampleforth is usually Abbot of Westminster, while a monk of Downside is Abbot of Glastonbury, and so on. Many of these medieval abbeys are in ruins or no longer exist – others are still in use as Church of England churches. The abbey of which I am Titular Abbot is a splendid church very much in use as the Anglican parish church and used by the famous public school of the same name. It is not very far from Downside, and the Sherborne match is one of Downside's most hotly-contested rugger fixtures. When I visited Sherborne some years ago and went round the abbey, I was invited to sign the Visitors' Book; and I could not resist signing myself 'J. R. Brookes, Abbot of Sherborne' – very naughty of me!

When I arrived in Rome in October 1966, to take up my new duties, I had to find somewhere to live. Theoretically, I could have lodged at the Abbey of Sant' Anselmo, which is the Benedictine Headquarters in Rome presided over by the Abbot Primate. However, it is an extremely cold building and I had been advised by Abbot Butler against staying there, so I turned to my old friends the Maryknoll Fathers at the Via Sardegna. With typical American hospitality, they very kindly welcomed me back and I lodged with them during the whole of the period I spent in Rome. Their house is pleasantly situated not far from the centre and very near the Borghese Gardens where I could go for a stroll when I needed a little exercise.

The work was not unduly onerous but enough to keep a middle-aged monk quite busy. I had to deal with every type of enquiry or petition from our 11 monasteries and 4 convents comprising some 500 monks and 100 nuns. This entailed dealing with the Abbot Primate at Sant' Anselmo and also with the various offices of the Vatican, mainly with the Sacred Congregation for Religious. Occasionally I was involved with pilgrimages in connection with such events as the Canonisation of the English Martyrs and that of Blessed Oliver Plunket. At such times life became very hectic. Needless to say, I was constantly being asked to find accommodation in Rome or to arrange audiences of the Holy Father, not only by my personal friends but also by those of our various houses who would be referred to me by the abbot or monk concerned. Rome is such an international city that people are always coming and going and I did not lack for visitors during my time there.

Very soon after my arrival in Rome, Abbot Butler was appointed Auxiliary Bishop in the Archdiocese of Westminster. It was not long after the appointment of Cardinal Heenan as Archbishop, and there had been a few people who had tipped Abbot Butler as an outsider for the post. It seemed very long odds at the time for a monk to be even considered but, after the death of Cardinal Heenan, Abbot Basil Hume of Ampleforth was appointed to succeed him – the first Benedictine to be Primate since before the Reformation. In modern times it is unusual for monks to be appointed to bishoprics as secular clergy would appear to be more suited to the pastoral work involved; but in medieval times it was commonplace as the secular clergy were with few exceptions almost totally uneducated.

Abbot Butler's elevation caused a vacancy and on the 28th December 1966, Dom Wilfrid Passmore was elected eighth Abbot of Downside. He was a 'cradle Catholic' and an OG, having been in the school when Abbot Trafford had been Headmaster. Although he took his Simple Vows a few days before my Solemn Profession in 1929, I did not know him very well as he went to Christ College, Cambridge in 1931, residing at Benet House, and after obtaining his degree went first to Sant' Anselmo in Rome and then to the University of Louvain to study Canon Law. On his return in 1938 he had a short spell as Prior of Worth and when Worth was closed for the duration of the War, he at last returned to Downside as Bursar. After the War he became Headmaster of Downside in 1946, a post which he held for 16 years. He was undoubtedly one of the great Headmasters and a keen admirer of Abbot Trafford, his own

Headmaster. Whereas the latter had put Downside on the social map, he put it firmly on the academic map. He knew that in the post-war years many parents suffered considerable hardship in order to provide their children with a public school education, and he was determined that the boys should realise this and work really hard so that their parents got their money's worth. At the end of his eight year term of office as Abbot, he did not stand for re-election because of ill-health, and he died two years later in 1976.

I normally remained in Rome for the Christmas and Easter holidays; but I went back to England each year for the long summer vacation. I would return to Downside and then make a round of the various houses to report to them in my capacity as Procurator in Curia and discuss any projects which they might wish me to undertake for them. I would also visit friends in England and usually end up in Northampton to see my close friend, Eric Phillips. For many years, Eric would take his annual holiday in September and we would travel to Italy together staying in Venice, after which I would return to Rome while Eric went back to Northampton. Eric had done a lot of work at Lourdes. Like myself, he was a Chaplain of the Knights of Malta and used to look after the English Knights at Lourdes. Through this he became friendly with the Duke Decaze who looked after the French Knights. The Duke, who had both French and Danish titles, had a splendid *Palazzo* in Venice and he invited Eric and myself to stay there. Our visit was such a success that we went there every autumn for 12 years in succession.

In 1969 I was invited back to Malta for the historic occasion when His Most Eminent Highness Fra Angelo de Mojana di Cologna, Prince and 77th Grand Master of the Knights of Malta, visited the Island. It was the first time a reigning Grand Master had been to Malta since the Knights were driven out by Napoleon in 1798 and his visit was celebrated in style. Maurice Dorman, who was still Governor General, gave a magnificent reception at San Anton on a Saturday evening; and then on the Sunday morning a Pontifical High Mass was celebrated by the Archbishop in St John's Cathedral during which the Grand Master occupied his traditional throne in the sanctuary. I was honoured by a place in the sanctuary and I well remember that the Mass was televised because we were all baked in the glare of the television lights. Afterwards I was present at a banquet given by the Archbishop.

It happened that my old friend from pre-war days at Ealing, Dom Adrian Morey, was visiting friends on the Island at the time; and I had the added pleasure of meeting him during my visit to Malta. He was then Headmaster of the Oratory School.

One of my former brethren, Dom Bernard Orchard, was also living in Rome for much of the time that I was there. We had been fellow Housemasters at Downside during the War; but afterwards Bernard went to our daughter house at Ealing and when the latter became independent he transferred his stability. He had two long spells as Headmaster of Ealing and then, being a Biblical scholar, came to Rome to continue his researches. We did not see a great deal of each other as we lived in different parts of the city and had different interests, but there is one story I must tell against myself. A great friend of mine who had been in the school came to Rome with his wife and put up at quite a good hotel near St Mary Major. They invited me to dinner in their hotel and also invited Dom Bernard. Just before dinner, our host told Bernard that I had remarked that the hotel was rather far from the centre of the city. Bernard immediately roared with laughter, saying: 'Oh yes! Definitely rather far out for a Guards Officer!' So you see, years after the Noviciate I was still being ribbed by my brethren for having been a Guardee!

Everyone knows that Rome has become a terrible place for bag-snatching, and I was mugged on one occasion. At Mary-knoll there was a tall iron outer gate to a small courtyard which I had gone through and closed behind me. I was just unlocking the inner door, when I heard someone knocking on the outer gate. I thought it might be one of the other priests returning, so I opened the gate to find a good looking well-dressed young man outside. He asked me if it were a *pensione* and I replied that it was a Priests' House; but that I knew all the *pensiones* in the district and offered to show him. As I stepped forward, he caught hold of the gold chain on which hung my pectoral cross and tugged. Fortunately, the cross was in my pocket and it stuck; but the chain broke and he dashed off with it to a car just down the street and drove off. I went at once to the Carabinieri, who sympathised but held out little hope of recovering my chain. For some reason it was one of the few times when I was wearing the very valuable cross which had belonged to Catharine of Braganza, so I was very relieved not to have lost this historic property of the monastery; but to be truthful I should have been even more distressed had I lost the cross given me by the boys of St Edward's.

In the course of my duties I met many diplomats in Rome and in particular the British Ministers to the Holy See. The British Government maintains two diplomatic missions in Rome: the British Embassy to the Italian State headed by an Ambassador and the British Legation to the Holy See headed by a Minister. The latter was only established in 1914. As a Protestant country, Britain has always been chary of recognising the Pope in any way; but at the outbreak of the Great War it was felt necessary to counteract the influence of the strongly Catholic Central European powers by establishing our own Representative at Rome. After the War it was continued, though there was considerable opposition and a stormy debate in Parliament.

His Majesty's first Envoy Extraordinary and Minister Plenipotentiary to the Holy See (to give him his full rather splendid title) had been a Catholic; but in view of the opposition from extreme Protestant groups it was felt more prudent that all future Ministers be non-Catholic so that there could be no question of divided loyalties. At the same time it was decided that the First Secretary (his Second-in-command) should be a Catholic, in order to advise the Minister on Catholic customs and protocol.

It is pleasant to record that, coincident with the historic and happy event of the Holy Father's visit to Britain last year, Her Majesty's Representative to the Holy See has been raised to the rank of Ambassador. Simultaneously, the Apostolic Delegate, the Pope's Representative in this country, has become a Papal Pro-Nuncio with full diplomatic status. It may be of interest that the doyen or Head of the Corps Diplomatique in any country is always the Ambassador who has been longest *en poste*, irrespective of how unimportant his country may be; but in Catholic countries the Papal Nuncio takes precedence.

In August 1970, Desmond Crawley relieved Sir Michael Williams as British Minister. I was in England on holiday at the time and it was not until the end of September and in rather sad circumstances that we met, but Desmond and his charming wife Daphne were to become very dear friends.

Although the First Secretary was always a Catholic, like the Minister he was a career diplomat who was moved every few years from post to post, so he could not be expected to be an expert on Rome or to have all the right contacts. For this reason Sir Francis D'Arcy Godolphin Osborne KCMG (later the Duke of Leeds), our Minister during the Second War, had appointed Jim Utley as Ecclesiastical Attaché, a local appointment which he held for very many years. Jim came from an old Yorkshire Catholic family and was a long time resident in Rome. He was invaluable to the many Ministers under whom he served as he knew everyone in Rome and was always able to introduce the Minister to the right person in any particular circumstance. I had first met him when we were both in Field Marshal Alex's entourage when he called on Pope Pius XII after the fall of Rome. Since being in Rome again as Procurator I had come to know him well and we were close friends.

Jim had a bachelor flat in the Chancery which was in the Via Condotti with a magnificent view up the famous Spanish Steps. He was the only person who lived there as the Minister resided and entertained in the Legation which was in the Via Bertoloni near the Borghese Gardens. Jim was due for retirement and had stayed on for a few weeks to see the new Minister in. Being a local appointment it was not pensionable but he qualified for a substantial gratuity on retirement after 25 years service. One Friday at the end of September, Desmond gave him a cheque for his gratuity which he paid into his bank account. That same night poor Jim suffered a massive heart attack and died all alone in his flat. Fortunately, someone came into the Chancery on the Saturday morning and saw the light still showing under the door, or he might not have been discovered until the Monday.

Jim had very few relatives, but one nephew was summoned

for the funeral and, on advice, Desmond notified Lord St Audries and his sister, the Honourable Maud Fuller-Acland-Hood, great friends of Jim's who had often visited him in Rome. Indeed I think Maudie had at one time wanted to marry him.

The First Secretary traced me to the Duke Decaze with whom I was staying in Venice. He told me that Monsignor Mostyn, a Canon of St Peter's, and very old friend of Jim's, would celebrate the Requiem Mass and asked if I would deliver the eulogy. I travelled back to Rome on the night sleeper, composing the eulogy on the way.

The Requiem was celebrated at St Sylvester's before a vast crowd of Jim's friends; and the Crawleys, whom I now met for the first time, kindly offered me a lift out to the cemetery. That evening they invited me to a cocktail party at the Legation, where the nephew and Maudie and her brother were staying.

The Canonisation of the Forty English Martyrs occurred at the end of the following month and I think I was able to be of considerable help to the Crawleys who had only been *en poste* for two months when this great event took place, and especially since poor Jim was no longer there to advise them. Peter Blackledge succeeded Jim as Ecclesiastical Attaché; but he also died of a heart attack after quite a short spell. After that there were no more appointments!

John Hunt and his first wife, Magdalen, came out for the Canonisation and stayed with the Crawleys. John and Desmond had been colleagues at the Commonwealth Office years before. I had known John when he was a Caverel House Prefect at Downside in 1938, the same year in which Peter Rawlinson, his friend and contemporary, had been both Head of Caverel and Head of School. John was destined to become Secretary to the Cabinet, one of the highest posts in the Civil Service. Like Peter, he has now become a noble Lord.

Besides the many English bishops who went to St Peter's for the ceremony dressed in their purple choir dress, the English Benedictine abbots also went in their black choir dress with cappa magna and black birettas. Amongst so much purple, the black stood out. As a titular abbot I had pectoral cross and ring but it would be unusual to wear a mitre or abbatial choir dress.

However, the other abbots asked me to join them on this festive occasion and the Abbot Primate kindly lent me his choir dress. There were Abbot Wilfrid Passmore of Downside, Abbot Basil Hume of Ampleforth (the future Cardinal Archbishop), Abbot Nicholas Holman of Fort Augustus Abbey and myself. I am told that we made quite an impressive quartet as we marched across St Peter's Square in our finery.

A year later on the Eve of Guy Fawkes Day, 4th November, 1971, I narrowly missed death or injury from an IRA bomb as did the Crawleys. I had dined with them at the Legation *en famille* and, a few minutes after they had seen me off, a small bomb placed on a window ledge in the street went off blasting right through the room, and the house, into the garden beyond. Desmond had just been seeing me off in this room and had an even narrower escape, as only two minutes before it went off he had turned out the lamps on each side of the very window outside which the bomb was lying.

It was said that the IRA were responsible but they never claimed it as they usually do and it is probable that it was planted by the local Red Brigade, on behalf of the IRA. It was the night after the IRA attack on the Post Office Tower in London and also the day before the Foreign Secretary was due to stay with the British Ambassador to Italy; but Desmond thought it was not a mistake and that he had been the target, as in the opinion of the IRA he was corrupting the mind of the Holy Father against the Catholics of Ireland. As is so often the case with acts of terrorism, the only victim of this bomb was an innocent passer-by who was blinded.

I have mentioned in the last chapter how Sir Maurice Dorman intervened in the matter of the Maltese Defence Agreement; and, though I thought I had finished with Maltese politics on leaving the Island, I now became involved in them once more.

Mintoff had come to power in 1971 and, although he and Archbishop Gonzi did not exactly see eye to eye, the latter avoided a head-on collision and was prepared to co-operate to a limited extent. Soon afterwards, the Archbishop came to Rome accompanied by his physician, Dr Farrugia, who was evidently a Mintoff man and later became the Maltese Ambassador to the

Holy See. The purpose was to discuss with Pope Paul the state of the Catholic Church in Malta now that Mintoff was in power. However, Mintoff was not on good terms with London, and he evidently asked the Archbishop to discuss certain points about the Defence Agreement with someone in authority in London if he had the opportunity.

The Archbishop stayed at a convent in Rome, and I naturally went to call upon my dear old friend. When he told me of his wish to make contact with London, I suggested that I introduce him to Desmond Crawley, and I arranged for us to have lunch at the Legation. In the event we stayed on there to dinner, as Desmond saw the importance of arranging a meeting for the Archbishop in London and sent off a telegram to the Foreign Office which resulted in a meeting being arranged with Ted Heath, the Prime Minister. Next day was a Sunday, and Desmond got the Archbishop an air ticket for London. Our intelligence must have been first rate, as half an hour later, a senior official at our Embassy to Italy telephoned Desmond to ask if he knew that Archbishop Gonzi was in Rome and had booked a flight to London that day!

The Archbishop duly saw the Prime Minister at Chequers and the following day he was invited to lunch with the Queen. She had become very fond of him at the time when she was a young naval wife in Malta, and took the trouble to return to London from Sandringham to meet him. I should perhaps add that the ubiquitous Dr Farrugia had refused to let the Archbishop speak to Desmond or myself alone and had presumably accompanied him when he saw Mr Heath; but when he tried to get himself invited to lunch with the Queen, he met with a very firm refusal.

Archbishop Gonzi came to Rome to see the Holy Father on a number of other occasions while I was there and we always met to talk of old times. Sometimes we lunched with the Crawleys who had become valued friends.

Very occasionally I had a private audience of the Holy Father; and on one of these occasions I plucked up all my courage and begged him a favour. I asked him to put the seal on my dear friend Michael Gonzi's long and faithful service to the Church by giving him a Cardinal's Hat. It would not only have been a

With a Swiss Guard at the Vatican

fitting reward to Michael Gonzi but also a tremendous boost to the Maltese people at a time when their Faith was being attacked and undermined by Mintoff and his supporters. Pope Paul smiled and promised to consider it, but I suppose there were other factors which weighed against it and it was not to be.

On 14th March 1973, I celebrated my 75th birthday, and the Crawleys very kindly gave a luncheon in my honour to which they invited many of our mutual friends. It was typical of their thoughtfulness. I have always been very sorry that Desmond never received the knighthood which he so richly deserved. In the past it was the custom that all Heads of Mission whether Ambassadors or Ministers were knighted. Just as I had been made an Abbot to lend prestige to my office, so knighthoods undoubtedly gave prestige to British diplomats. However Harold Wilson's Socialist Government decided to cut the number of knighthoods for the Diplomatic Service by two thirds, so that only one in three would get one. As a result, Desmond was the very first Minister to the Holy See not to be knighted and this must have been quite embarassing for him, as both Italians and others could not understand it.

I took the Crawleys on many excursions in and around Rome to such places as Monte Cassino and Anzio. At the latter place we visited the British War Cemetery and quite by chance Daphne came across the grave of an officer in the Scots Guards who had been a childhood friend of hers. She knew he had been killed in Italy but had no idea where he was buried. He had only been 21.

I was very sad when the Crawleys' tour finished and they left Rome in May 1975. Desmond was succeeded by Dugald Malcolm, a former officer in the Argyll and Sutherland Highlanders.

As I have mentioned, Abbot Passmore did not stand for re-election at the end of his term of office and on 17th December 1974, Dom John Roberts was elected ninth Abbot of Downside and is still in office. I have spoken earlier about my friend Wulstan Phillipson who was one of my fellow novices, and of his slight weakness for the delights of the table. He was also very conservative even to the extent of preferring quite lawfully to continue to offer his daily private Mass in accordance with the old Tridentine rite. When this abbatial election came up he was very worried that perhaps one of the younger monks would be elected who might introduce many unwelcome changes. My guess is that he cast his vote for Dom John but in any case he was delighted that the latter was elected. Breakfast in the monastic refectory at Downside used to be a rather splendid affair. Not only was there a choice of porridge and cereals, but this could be followed by eggs cooked in various ways, bacon, sausages, etc, finished off with toast and marmalade. Abbot Roberts felt that this was too luxurious to be in keeping with monastic poverty and one of his first actions was to abolish the cooked breakfast, though a simple boiled egg could still be specially ordered by the weaker brethren. Wulstan, who enjoyed his bacon and eggs, was very put out and reproached the Abbot, whereupon the latter replied, 'Ah well – you elected me!' Dear Wulstan has gone to his reward; but he had a tremendous sense of humour and I am sure he would enjoy my telling this story against him. In fact it illustrates very well the way in which monks with the guidance of the Holy Spirit elect the best man for the job, and then for the next eight years they have to accept his decisions, which is of course very good for us. Wanting to have one's own way is a most human failing and accepting instead the will of a superior is probably one of the most difficult aspects of monastic life.

In July 1975 Blessed Oliver Plunkett was canonised. This was primarily an Irish occasion, but I was very much involved because Downside have the Saint's bones in a reliquary in the Abbey church. Furthermore as he was the last Catholic to suffer for the Faith at Tyburn, there was considerable interest among English Catholics.

Dom John, my Abbot, came out to Rome with a small party of monks, boys, and some parents. They stayed out at Ostia and on the day of the Canonisation it poured with rain all the way into Rome. However, no sooner had they descended from their coach in St Peter's Square than the rain stopped and there was brilliant sunshine all through the long ceremony which, unlike the Canonisation of the English Martyrs, was held on the steps outside St Peter's so that the vast square could be filled with far more pilgrims than could get inside the Basilica. After the ceremony the Pope appeared at his window overlooking the square and led the Angelus. No sooner had he finished than the Heavens opened and the deluge came down. I like to think that by holding back the rain during the ceremony, St Oliver performed a small miracle on his own Canonisation Day.

My own dear Abbot is such a humble man that he wanted to go with the boys into the ordinary stand in which they had reserved seats; and I had some difficulty in persuading him that he must join the other VIPs in their stand near the Altar.

In 1977 the 1st Battalion Irish Guards were stationed in West Germany and they asked the Grand Duke of Luxembourg to present the Shamrock and take the salute on St Patrick's Day. They also did me the honour of asking me to conduct the service before the parade and very kindly sent me my return ticket from Rome and put me up in the Officers' Mess which I much enjoyed. During the War, the Grand Duke's mother had reigned as Grand Duchess in her own right and like so many foreign royalty had taken refuge with her family in England. Prince Jean was only a boy and was sent to Ampleforth after which he joined the Irish Guards. He was sent to the Guards Depot like any other potential officer as 'Recruit Luxembourg, J'. He went on to Sandhurst and was duly commissioned into the Regiment, finishing up as Captain Prince Jean of Luxembourg. He has always been immensely proud of his service in the Regiment; and the most popular photograph displayed in hotels and restaurants in Luxembourg is that of him in the uniform of an Irish Guards captain.

Our host on this occasion was the Commanding Officer, Lieutenant Colonel James Baker. He noticed that I had lost my beloved blackthorn stick which I had carried all through the war and, a few weeks after my return to Rome, a brand new blackthorn arrived with a silver band beautifully inscribed to commemorate the occasion. I was most touched. I have become a little lame in recent years and I carry my blackthorn everywhere and find it invaluable.

The Procurator in Curia is normally appointed by the General Chapter when it meets every four years. In 1973 after seven years in Rome I was a little doubtful about carrying on but Abbot Passmore encouraged me to do so, and I was therefore Procurator for 11 years, finally leaving Rome in 1977.

I was asked to go to Colwich Abbey in Staffordshire as Chaplain to the nuns in place of Dom Aidan Trafford, the brother of Abbot Trafford, who had been there for 13 years and was now unwell. I duly took up this new post in the autumn of 1977.

Chapter 17

Epilogue

As far back as the time of St Benedict himself and his sister St Scholastica, there have been Benedictine nuns as well as monks. In pre-Reformation times there were numerous Benedictine abbeys and priories of nuns in England – Romsey Abbey in Hampshire and Great St Helen's whose Priory church still stands in the City of London, to name but two; although, unlike our present age when women religious far outnumber men, in medieval times the monks and friars were far more numerous than the nuns.

In 1607 a handful of exiled Englishmen founded St Gregory's monastery at Douai in Flanders, thus establishing the first house of English Benedictines since the Reformation; and it was this house which was driven from France back to England at the time of the French Revolution and established itself at Downside in 1814. Downside is thus the oldest and senior house of the English Congregation, though Ampleforth have the distinction that in 1607 Dom Sigebert Buckley, the last surviving monk of Westminster, aggregated Dom Robert Sadler and Dom Edward Mayhew, two young English monks of the Cassinese Congregation, to his Abbey of Westminster, thus perpetuating an unbroken link with that house and with the ancient pre-Reformation English Congregation. Another handful of exiles had started monastic life in 1608 with the foundation of St Lawrence's at Dieulouard in France; and in 1613 Dom Edward Mayhew joined them. Like St Gregory's, they were driven out of France at the Revolution and returned to England, finally settling at Ampleforth in 1802.

At Downside, 1983

214

In 1625 the monks at Douai founded the first house for Benedictine nuns since the Reformation at Cambrai in Flanders with nine young Englishwomen. This house flourished and also returned to England at the time of the Revolution, eventually establishing itself at Stanbrook in 1838. Three nuns of this house left Cambrai in 1651 and, with the generous help of Charles I's French Queen Henrietta Maria, made a new foundation in Paris under the patronage of Our Lady of Good Hope. Like very many other communities, this house was driven out of France during the Revolution and eventually settled at Colwich in 1836.

The first Prioress in Paris was Dame Bridget More, a great great granddaughter of St Thomas. Just as the ordained monks are prefixed 'Dom' so the choir nuns are prefixed 'Dame' and this ancient custom, which is unique to Benedictines, has continued to the present time. In the same way, just as an abbot is addressed formally as 'My Lord Abbot', an abbess is addressed as 'My Lady Abbess'.

The nuns were strictly enclosed, though this has been slightly relaxed in recent times; and, like the monks, their main occupation is the *Opus Dei*. I did not take part in this but celebrated the Conventual Mass for them in the Abbey church every day at 8.30am, and on Thursdays and Sundays I gave them Benediction of the Blessed Sacrament at 5pm. I also heard their confessions. Though not a public church, local Catholics came to Mass particularly on Sundays and though there were no set times I often heard their confessions as well.

The house was warm enough but the Abbey church was unheated and I suffered greatly from the cold in winter. To combat this, the nuns had a special silver-plated hand-warmer which they filled with hot water and placed on the altar, so that I could pause at convenient moments during the Mass and warm my frozen hands.

I had a small suite in the house but outside the enclosure, comprising a bedroom and a sitting room. There were some guest rooms and I took my meals in the guests' dining room. The nuns cooked the meals inside the enclosure and in the old days the food had to be passed through the 'turn', a sort of turntable hatch. A lay Housekeeper called Miss Giusso served me and any other guests who were staying in the house.

There was a small cottage in the grounds which had been intended for the Chaplain. I believe my predecessor, Dom Aidan, had occupied it but, as he became infirm, it was decided to move him into the house, and the cottage had been let to a Mr and Mrs Morrissey, the latter being a sister of one of the nuns, Dame Gertrude Baker. They had a daughter called Trudy with whom I became great friends. Later she wrote to me at Downside; and it is just as well the letter was not opened by the Abbot, as she addressed me as 'My darling Dolly' . . . However I was by then 80 years of age so I do not suppose he would have minded!

As readers can see, the duties were not onerous; and I found the life rather lonely. I was always a great walker and I went for many long walks in the surrounding countryside, but the evenings hung heavily after the rather early evening meal, particularly in the summer. There was a very pleasant pub called the 'Lamb and Flag' near the canal and I got into the habit of visiting it most evenings. I seldom drink alcohol but I came to an arrangement with the barmaid that when I asked for 'the usual', she would give me a tonic water with a slice of lemon which looked, of course, like a gin and tonic. I found the company very congenial and I soon came to be accepted as one of the regulars.

The Right Reverend Dame Frances Wilcox was the Abbess, and I cannot pretend that we got on too well. My great friend was the Prioress, Dame Edith Street, who could not have been kinder to me.

I must tell a little story against myself. On one occasion I went up to London to christen the grandchild of a very old friend, and I borrowed an alarm clock from the Abbess, as I like to be able to wake myself and say my Office before the household is stirring when I am staying with friends. Stupidly, I forgot to pack it when I left. On my return to Colwich I telephoned my hostess to thank her at once before writing my 'bread and butter' letter, and she told me I had left the alarm clock but she had it safely and would post it on. I was overcome with confusion for being such a nuisance – I always think it is an unforgivable thing for a guest to forget some item which has to be sent on – so I at once told her not to bother to send it on, that it did not matter in the least and that I would collect it next time I was in London. A few hours later I had to telephone her again and eat my words, begging her to return the clock to me with the utmost urgency as it was one of the Lady Abbess's most prized possessions, having been presented to her by the Community on some important occasion!

One of the problems of being a chaplain to nuns is that they rely upon you for Mass, and it is therefore very difficult to go away, as you have to arrange for someone else to say Mass for you. I had such occasions as St Patrick's Day which I liked to spend with my old Regiment and there were many friends who were always asking me to come and baptize a child or grand-child. It was rather embarrassing having to ask the local clergy to do my duty for me, though I was fortunate in having the Dominican friars of Hawksyard Priory not far away and very helpful.

Thus, although the Abbess and the other nuns had been very kind to me, I was not sorry when Dom Columba Thorne was sent to relieve me early in January 1979, and I returned once more to Downside.

I had not been resident at Downside since I left to rejoin the Army as a Chaplain in 1942, nearly 40 years earlier. On the face of it, it might seem that I should be classed by St Benedict with those monks he so disapproved of who had no stability and were ever roaming; but of course all my postings had in fact been under obedience to my various Abbots.

I am now living in retirement with no set duties other than to live the Rule as best I can and to act as one of the school confessors. I still love to be with young people and I take every opportunity of attending events in the school such as plays and debates. My old friend, Dom Denis Agius, who was Junior Housemaster for 18 years, has retired from that job but still has a room in the school where he looks after a section of boys who have private rooms. Most evenings he invites me to come up after dinner and have cocoa with him and there are usually a number of boys who join us for long talks on all sorts of topics.

I have always suffered from the cold and, although the Abbey church and monastery are quite well heated, I have been excused from the long Conventual High Mass, and instead I say my little private Mass in Latin in the Crypt chapel which is warmly heated. The young monks are very kind to me, preparing the altar, laying out the vestments, and usually one of them serves my Mass. The Rule says very touchingly, 'Reverence the seniors, love the juniors,' and there is indeed a charming respect for the elderly monks on the part of the youngsters, while I think I can truly claim that the older monks do indeed 'love the juniors' and do their utmost to help them progress and persevere in the religious life.

I have in this book quoted what are I hope appropriate parts of the Rule of St Benedict; and I cannot do better than end by quoting the last paragraph of the Prologue to the Holy Rule:

'We have, therefore, to establish a school for the Lord's service, in the setting forth of which we hope to order nothing that is harsh or rigorous. But if anything be somewhat strictly laid down, according to the dictates of sound reason, for the amendment of vices or the preservation of charity, do not therefore fly in dismay from the way of salvation, whose beginning cannot but be strait and difficult. But as we go forward in our life and in faith, we shall with hearts enlarged and unspeakable sweetness of love run in the way of God's commandments; so that never departing from His guidance, but persevering in His teaching in the monastery until death, we may by patience share in the sufferings of Christ, that we may deserve to be partakers of His Kingdom. Amen.'

Index

221